LIVERPOOL IN 1840.—BLACK BALL PACKET DISEMBARKING PASSENGERS.

By courtesy of T. H. Parker, 12a Berkeley Street, London, W. 1.

[Frontispiece.

THE
WESTERN OCEAN
PACKETS

BY
BASIL LUBBOCK

DOVER PUBLICATIONS, INC.
New York

Dedicated to the Western Ocean Traveller.

This Dover edition, first published in 1988, is an unabridged, slightly corrected republication of the work originally published by James Brown & Son (Glasgow) Ltd., Glasgow, in 1925. The illustration of "House Flags" on the back cover originally appeared facing p. 120, and has been reduced in size. Certain illustrations have been moved from their original positions in this edition in order to maximize space.

Manufactured in the United States of America
Dover Publications, Inc.
31 East 2nd Street
Mineola, N.Y. 11501

Library of Congress Cataloging-in-Publication Data

Lubbock, Basil.
  The Western Ocean packets.

  Reprint. Originally published: Glasgow : J. Brown & Son, 1925.
  Includes index.
  1. Packets—United States—History—19th century. 2. United States—History, Naval—To 1900. 3. Navigation—United States—History—19th century. I. Title.
VK23.L8   1988   387.2′43′0973   88-3814
ISBN 0-486-25684-7 (pbk.)

PREFACE

A few years ago I wrote a series of articles on the
Western Ocean Packets in the *Nautical Magazine*.
Several readers expressed a wish that these should be
published in book form. In this little book I have
complied with their request whilst taking the opportunity to add somewhat to the original matter.

The famous American packet ships, though their
day was not a long one, played a very big part in the
making of a nation—a nation which, by its sheer
virility and heroic energy, by its superb strength of
brain and muscle, has, at the present day, become one
of the most, if not the most, important factor in this
world's development along the lines of steady progress,
whether moral or physical.

If Jonathan already had a backbone, a sturdy
Anglo-Saxon backbone, upon which I venture to hope
he will ever continue to rely, these gallant, hard-sailed
packets with their 'tween-decks crowded with emigrants,
were the first to put meat on his bones, to fill out his
clothes and add weight to his muscle and breadth to
his stature.

But, in conveying their multitude of nationalities
across the stormy Atlantic, these ships did far more

than populate a continent or develop a great nation; they gave a chance to the underling, to the ignoramus, to the down-trodden, to the half-starved and to the tyrant-ridden to become self-respecting, self-supporting citizens of the world.

Individualism, not socialism or communism, has made the great United States of America.

It was the grit in the individual unit, that made him face the indescribable hardships of the passage across the Western Ocean and take advantage of the opportunities offering in a land, which stout-hearted pioneers had barely scratched.

Not only America but Europe has good cause to be grateful to these valiant little packet ships, with their self-reliant captains, heavy-fisted mates and hard-bitten crews.

And in writing this sketch of their history, I hope to contribute my mite towards keeping their memory green.

CONTENTS

PART I.

vii

CONTENTS

PART II.

CONTENTS

ILLUSTRATIONS

xi

THE
WESTERN OCEAN
PACKETS

The Western Ocean Packets.

PART I.

In the Black Ball Line I served my time:
    Hooraw for the Black Ball Line.

There's Liverpool Pat with his tarpaulin hat:
    Amelia, whar' you bound to?
And Yankee John, the packet rat,
    Across the Western Ocean.

Beware those packet ships, I pray:
    Amelia, whar' you bound to?
They steal your stores and clothes away
    Across the Western Ocean.

" O good-morning, Mister Tapscott."
    "Good-morn, my gal," says he.
" O, it's have you got a packet ship
    For to carry me over the sea?"

" Oh, yes I have a packet ship
    She's called the *Henry Clay*:
She lies down at the North Pier Head
    A-taking in her mail."   (*Old Chanties.*)

DURING the first half of the nineteenth century, the Atlantic Ferry was almost entirely in the hands of the Americans. The little sailing ship, heading the newspaper shipping columns, advertised the departures and arrivals of famous Black Ball, Swallow Tail, Black Star, Red Star, and Black X Packets, American every one of them. And it was not until 1840 that the first of the present great steamship

1

lines, the Cunard, entered the arena with the steamship *Britannia*, whose average speed was only 8½ knots and coal consumption a bare 38 tons per day. For many years after that date the Yankee packet was Lord of the Western Ocean.

Dickens crosses on the " George Washington."

Dickens, it will be remembered, preferred to return from America in the Swallow Tail packet, *George Washington*, rather than undergo a second experience in a British smoke-box. One can well imagine the magnificent line of tall packets, which he describes, lying along the waterfront below Wall Street, their bowsprits crossing the roadway and stabbing at the windows of the houses opposite. It is possible that he witnessed the enviable sight of a packet coming up to her berth under sail, for, though tugboats were instituted in 1835, their charges were so excessive and their power so feeble that ships never used them except when it was absolutely necessary.

" Ship Sense."

In those days ships were looked upon as being alive and more than human. "Ship sense" were words in common use; and it was commonly said, and often seriously believed, that an old Western Ocean traveller could find her way from the Mersey River to her own pier in New York without man's help. This calls to mind the old sailor's story of the famous *Dreadnought*. How after several days of thick fog and with the weather still as thick as pea soup, Captain Samuels came on

deck and said to his mate: "I guess we must be there
or tharabouts." And how a moment later the great
flier bumped gently up against her own pier in the
East River.

It is even stated by American historians that these
proud packet ship captains were accustomed to sail
right away from the dock side when the wind served.

The manœuvre is thus described: All plain sail being
set, the yards were laid flat aback, the lines being
eased off as the vessel was backed stern first into the
stream amidst the cheers of the spectators. Then as
soon as he had sea room and a clear course, the captain
put his helm over, swung his yards and trimmed away
for sea.

The Black Ball Line.

The first and the best known of the packet lines
was the notorious Black Ball, renowned all over the
world for smart passages and fighting officers. This
line began to run between New York and Liverpool in
1816 with four little 500-ton ships—the *Amity*, *Courier*,
Pacific and *James Monroe*.

These vessels were at once admitted to be a great
advance on the old style go-as-you-please Western
Ocean waggon. Their sailing day was the first of the
month, and neither weather nor lack of freight was
allowed to interfere with this rule: they were driven,
not allowed to loaf, across the Western Ocean; in
addition to this they were far superior in cabin arrange-
ments and general equipment.

The Accommodation of the "Pacific."

The newspapers of the day devoted a great deal of space to advertising the spaciousness of their cabins and the beauty of their decoration; for instance, the *Liverpool Courier* thus describes the cabins of the *Pacific*:—"Her dining room is 40 feet by 14. A mahogany table runs down the centre, with seats on each side formed of the same wood and covered with black haircloth. The end of the dining-room aft is spanned by an elliptical arch, supported by handsome pillars of Egyptian porphyry. The sides of the cabin are formed of mahogany and satinwood, tastefully disposed in panels and most superbly polished. The doors of the staterooms are very neat, the compartments in each being inlaid with a square of plate glass. An arch extends over the entrance to each room, supported by delicate pillars of beautiful white Italian marble, exquisitely polished. The staterooms are seven on each side; they are fitted up with much taste, and with a studious regard for the comfort and convenience of the passengers."

These ships were built of live oak and copper fastened, but their bottoms were not coppered until they reached Liverpool. The coppering of American and Canadian ships was usually done at Liverpool; in fact, many a new ship was sent across the Atlantic on her maiden trip for this sole reason.

"ALBION."

By courtesy of T. H. Parker, 12a Berkeley Street, London W.1.

"FIDELIA"

By courtesy of the "Nautical Magazine."

Hard Driving makes Good Records but Short Lives.

In six months the *William Thompson*, *James Cropper*, *New York* and *Orbit* were added to the four pioneer ships, giving a further service sailing from New York on the 16th of the month. These were soon followed by the *Nestor*, *Albion*, *Canada* and *Columbia*.

The average passage of the Black Ball ships during the first nine years of the firm's existence was 23 days eastward bound and 40 days going to the westward. The best trip was made by the *Canada*, which reached Liverpool on one occasion in 15 days 18 hours.

This meant hard driving and such sail carrying against the westerlies on the return trips that none of these early ships lasted more than a few years.

Herman Melville describes the Change from Packet Ship to Whaler.

According to Herman Melville these early ships very often found their future amongst the Nantucket and New Bedford whaling fleet. He describes the transition in his own inimitable way in his first book *Redburn*, and as this book is now very scarce the quotation should be of interest:—

"Aboard of those liners the crew have terrible hard work, owing to their carrying such a press of sail, in order to make as rapid passages as possible and sustain the ship's reputation for speed. Hence it is, that although they are the very best of sea-going craft and built in the best possible manner, and with the very best materials, yet a few years of scudding before the wind, as they do, seriously impairs their constitutions— like robust young men who live too fast in their teens— and they are soon sold out for a song: generally to the people of Nantucket, New Bedford and Sag Harbour, who repair and fit them out for the whaling business.

"Thus, the ship that once carried over-gay parties of ladies and gentlemen, as tourists, to Liverpool or London, now carries a crew of harpooners round Cape Horn into the Pacific. And the mahogany and bird's-eye maple cabin which once held rosewood card tables and brilliant coffee urns, and in which many a bottle of champagne and many a bright eye sparkled, now accommodates a bluff Quaker from Martha's Vineyard; who, perhaps, while lying with his ship in the Bay of Islands, New Zealand, entertains a party of naked chiefs and savages at dinner, in place of the packet captain doing the honours to the literati, theatrical stars, foreign princes, and gentlemen of leisure and fortune, who generally talked gossip, politics and nonsense across the table, in trans-Atlantic trips."

Captain Charles H. Marshall.

From its very start, the Black Ball Line prospered and there is little doubt that it owed its success to its captains in the early days and to its capable manager when competition was fiercest.

Charles H. Marshall began his sea career in the whaler *Lima* of Nantucket. Nine years later he obtained his first command, the *Julius Caesar*.

In 1835 Captain Charles H. Marshall, having commanded in turn the packets *James Cropper*, *Britannia* and *South America*, became managing owner of the line. He died in 1865, but the firm was continued by his son under the name of H. C. Marshall & Co. until the early eighties. By that time it was found impossible to compete any longer with the steamers, and, like most of the other sailing packet lines, the Black Ball sold their ships and retired from business.

" Fidelia," Clipper of the Black Ball Fleet.

The ships gradually were increased in size from 500 up to 1500 tons; amongst the best known were the *Montezuma*, *Yorkshire*, *Isaac Wright*, *Isaac Webb*, *Manhattan*, *Harvest Queen*, *Great Western*, *North America* and *England*. The clipper of the fleet was the *Fidelia*, which ran from New York to the North-West Lightship in 13 days 7 hours, and from the N.W. Lightship to Sandy Hook in 17 days 6 hours.

The *Fidelia* was a typical packet ship of 969 tons register, her best known commander being Captain W. G. Furber. She was built by the celebrated William H. Webb of New York, who was responsible not only for many of the finest packet ships but also for a goodly number of America's fastest clippers.

The Black Ball Colours.

The great distinguishing mark carried by a Black Ball packet was the large black ball, sewn or painted on her fore topsail; this made her very easy to pick out from a crowd of ships underweigh. The idea was copied by several other packet ship firms, though I don't think it was ever used outside the Atlantic passenger trade.

The Black X ships always sported a large black X in their fore topsails, Enoch Train put a T in his fore topsail, whilst the famous *Dreadnought* always wore a blood-red cross like a Crusader, because she belonged to the St. George's Cross Line.

According to Captain Clark the early Black Ballers were painted black from the waterline up with bright bands, scraped and varnished; this was the usual colour scheme of American ships in the early days of the nineteenth century. He also states that their boats, deck houses and bulwarks were painted green.

The later ships seem to have been painted man-of-war fashion, hulls *a la* Nelson, black with black ports on white strake; poop and deck houses white; lower masts and yards, bowsprit, spanker gaff and boom and spencer gaff white; jibbooms, upper masts and spars black.

The Red Star Line.

In the year 1821 Messrs. Byrnes, Grimble & Co. inaugurated the Red Star Line of Liverpool packets with the *Manhattan*, *Hercules*, *Panther* and *Meteor*, sailing on the 24th of the month from New York.

The Swallow Tail Line.

The Red Star Line was closely followed by the Swallow Tail Line (Messrs. Fish, Grinnell & Co., afterwards Grinnell, Minturn & Co.). Their first ships were the *Napoleon*, *Silas Richards*, *York* and *George*. They sailed on the 8th and completed the weekly service from New York.

This line was not long content to run to Liverpool only, but in 1823 built four little 400-ton ships—the *Corinthian*, *Cortes*, *Brighton* and *Columbia*—for the London trade. Later again, when the Californian gold rush began, they started a line of clipper ships round the Horn, three of the most celebrated of these being the *Flying Cloud*, *Sea Serpent* and *Three Brothers* (now a coal hulk at Gib.) Many a famous packet sailed under the Swallow Tail house-flag. Most of them were built in New York by Westervelt; a few, however, came from Damariscotta and Boston. Like the Black Ballers, they rarely exceeded 1500 tons, and were very strongly built of hacmatack and oak, with three decks, rather full lines and plenty of beam.

The first additions to their Liverpool line were the *Roscoe*, *Independence*, *George Washington* and *Pennsylvania*. *Roscoe's* commander was the famous Capt. Joseph C. Delano, of New Bedford, who was afterwards so successful with *Patrick Henry*. *Independence* (Captain Ezra Nye), 734 tons, built in 1834 by Smith & Dimon, was a very fast ship and a great rival of the Black Ball *Montezuma*, built the following year by Brown & Bell, and some 300 tons larger. Both vessels earned renown by doing the eastward run in fourteen days, and that more than once. The *George Washington*, of course, will ever be associated with the name of Dickens. On the Dickens passage she beat the Cunarder by 29 hours.

The Dramatic Line.

In the late thirties Captain E. K. Collins, who afterwards gave his name to the Collins Line of steamers, established the Dramatic Line of sailing packets to Liverpool as rivals to the Swallow Tail Line. His first ships were the *Shakespeare*, Captain John Collins; the *Siddons*, Captain N. B. Palmer (afterwards the commander of the famous Yankee tea clipper *Oriental*); the *Sheridan*, Captain de Peyster, and the *Roscius*, Captain Asa Eldridge. These vessels were all built by Brown & Bell of New York, and registered 895 tons, being thus considerably bigger than any other packets at that date.

The Dimensions of the " Roscius."

The following dimensions of the *Roscius* approximate closely to those of the other ships:—Burthen 1100 tons; length of main deck, 170 feet; length of spar deck, 180 feet; beam 36½ feet; depth of hold 22 feet; height of cabin, 6½ feet; height from keelson to main truck, 187 feet; length of mainyard, 75 feet.

Packet Ship Racing in 1836 and 1837.

With the advent of the Dramatic Line, the number of packet ships sailing between New York and Liverpool was increased from 16 to 20, with a total tonnage of about 14,000 tons. Besides these there were packets running to London and Havre, as well as Cope's Line from Philadelphia to Liverpool; these added another 20 ships at least to the packet fleet.

The Dramatic Line were advertised to sail on the same

day from New York as the Swallow Tail, and other packets often clashed with the Black Ball, so that for the first time the ships found themselves racing against each other.

Race between " Columbus," " George Washington," and " Sheffield."

The first packet ship race of any note was that between the *Columbus*, 597 tons, Captain Palmer, the *George Washington* (734 tons), Captain Henry Holdridge, of the Swallow Tail Line, and the *Sheffield*, Captain Allen.

These three ships left New York on the 8th July, 1836, in the midst of a crowd of other vessels, all bound for Liverpool. We are told that heavy betting on the result of the race took place in New York. The racing packets were in company on the Banks of Newfoundland but did not meet again. The *George Washington* was the first to signal Holyhead, followed two or three hours later by the *Sheffield*. Both ships arrived in the Mersey on the afternoon of the 25th, 17 days out.

The *Columbus* arrived on the following morning.

Race between "Columbus" and "Sheridan."

In 1837 the fast little *Columbus* challenged the new Dramatic liner *Sheridan*, which was about to sail on her maiden trip to Liverpool. A stake of 20,000 dollars a side was speedily arranged, and both ships were carefully prepared for the contest. The big *Sheridan* managed to collect a picked crew of 40 men by

offering pay at 25 dollars a month and a bonus of 50
dollars a man provided she won the race.

Captain Clark in *The Clipper Ship Era* states that
both ships sailed together on 2nd February, 1837, and
that the *Columbus* was first home in 16 days, followed
by the *Sheridan* two days later.

By choosing the 8th of the month as their sailing
day, the Dramatic Line were more to be feared by the
Swallow Tail than by the Black Ball.

Grinnell and Minturn's "Patrick Henry."

Grinnell, Minturn & Co. replied to the challenge
by launching in 1839 the 1000-ton ship *Patrick Henry*.
She was given in charge of their veteran captain, J. C.
Delano.   Under his guidance she is said to have made
more money for her tonnage than any other ship in their
service.   She was built by Brown & Bell, and soon
proved her title to be enrolled amongst the élite few
who had crossed the Atlantic in 14 days.

"Ashburton."

Their next ship of note was the *Ashburton*, of
1015 tons, commanded by Captain Henry Huttleston,
of New Bedford, and built in 1843.   She was also a
very fast ship and once made the passage from New
York in 12 days.

"The Famous Henry Clay."

She was followed by the *Henry Clay*, of 1250
tons, a vessel which was the subject of a well-known
chanty.   One of the first three-deckers, she caused quite

a sensation in New York, and as she lay loading at her pier, No. 18 East River, opposite Grinnell & Minturn's office, the crowd of admirers round her became so great as to seriously interfere with the stevedores. The *Henry Clay* had two lives, for, after being burnt, her charred hulk was bought and rebuilt by Spofford & Tileston in 1852, and she afterwards ran for many years in their Liverpool Line.

The "New World," built by Donald McKay.

But perhaps the most noted of all the Swallow Tail ships was the *New World*. She measured 1400 tons, and was reckoned the largest and finest ship in the American Merchant Marine in 1846, the date of her launch. She was one of the first vessels built by the famous Donald McKay; and was ordered by her first master, Captain William Skiddy, who, however, sold the greater part of his interest in her to Messrs. Grinnell, Minturn & Co. About this time, owing to the Irish famine, the packets were receiving as much as 5s. a barrel freight money on flour. The *New World*, on her arrival in Liverpool, caused almost as much attention as she had done in New York, and received the honour of a visit from the Prince Consort. After running to Liverpool for many years, she ended her days in Grinnell & Minturn's London Line.

The "Cornelius Grinnell."

The next ship built by Donald McKay for the Swallow Tail Line was the *Cornelius Grinnell*, launched in 1850. She was not quite such a big ship as the

New World, her chief measurements being:—Length on the keel, 172 feet; length on deck, 180 feet; beam 38 feet; depth of hold $23\frac{1}{2}$ feet; her main lower mast was 84 feet long and her mainyard 74 feet. She had a full poop, 80 feet long and a topgallant foc'sle. Her registered tonnage worked out at about 1100 tons.

In the Appendix I give some details of her specification taken from an account in the *Illustrated London News* of 31st August, 1850, at which date she was lying in the London Docks, having just arrived on her maiden passage. This account is interesting not only as showing the strength of the vessel but as an example of what is almost a dead art, namely, wooden shipbuilding.

The Black X Line of London Packets.

As important and as famous as either the Black Ball or the Swallow Tail, the Black X Line of packets, founded by John Griswold in the early twenties, ran only to London. Its first ships were the *Sovereign*, *Cambria*, *President* and *Hudson*, this last the first command of E. E. Morgan, the famous shipmaster who afterwards became manager and chief owner of the line.

Captain E. E. Morgan.

There are many anecdotes told of Morgan. H was noted for the calm, unruffled way in which he took the trials of a packet captain's life. Instead of the usual flare-up of sea blessings, he would treat the mate who had neglected his duty to a sardonic "Never mind; I'll attend to it myself this voyage." He was at his best when the weather was at its worst, and the sight of him,

swaying easily to the heave of the ship and chewing
steadily at an unlighted cigar, put confidence into many
a frightened emigrant. On one such occasion he so
impressed Leslie, the artist, who, with Thackeray,
happened to be making a trip as far as the Wight in
Morgan's ship, that Leslie straightway made a sketch
of the captain hailing the men aloft through his
hollowed hands.   With the exclamation, "Great
heavens, what a picture !" the artist dodged under the
lee of the weather bulwark and dashed off a portrait of
his skipper, which is now a treasured possession of
Morgan's family.

One of the great games of the early Victorian period,
especially on shipboard, was the game of draughts, at
which Morgan specially prided himself.   A bad draught
player could do what neither an indifferent mate nor a
gale of wind could do, he could stir the old captain into
a temper.   Yet in the days when the generality of sea
captains were inclined to be rough sea-bears, Morgan
was the equal of any courtier on an occasion of ceremony.
When Queen Victoria lunched on board the famous
Black X liner, which had been called after her, the
Duke of Newcastle, who was one of the guests, asked
Morgan why he had never called one of the vessels after
Her Majesty before.   "Because," replied Morgan,
suavely, "we never before built a ship that was worthy
of her."

The Black X Packet "Victoria."

This *Victoria* created more sensation at her
launch than any of the present day floating hotels,

however huge and luxurious. She was built in the year 1844, measured 1000 tons, and was one of the first packets to have a long poop stretching forward of the mainmast; besides which her second class passengers rejoiced in a "house on deck"—what in a modern wind-jammer would be called the midship-house—instead of having to stew in the ill-ventilated 'tween decks.

A Winter Passage in the "Hendrick Hudson."

When the Black X on an American cotton fore topsail was first seen in the Thames, the packets did not exceed 500 tons. But from the first they were noted for their fine wedge-shaped models and weatherly qualities. They were easily distinguishable amongst the crowded shipping of the London River, on account of their short lower masts, unusually square yards, big blocks and grassrope running gear. R. C. Leslie in his *Old Sea Wings, Ways and Words* says that there was a great look of the Dutchman or Souwegian about these little ships, which is only natural when one remembers that they were mostly built in New Jersey, at that time almost a Swedish colony.

Leslie in his *Waterbiography* gives a very interesting account of his passage from New York to London in the *Hendrick Hudson*. This vessel was built at New York in 1841, and launched, ready for sea with masts stepped and yards crossed, in 89 days from the date of laying the keel. It was on 21st November, 1842, that she left New York with Leslie on board. The ship was in charge of a smart young captain, but she was

"VICTORIA."

By courtesy of the "Nautical Magazine."

" EUROPE."

By courtesy of the P.S.N. Co.

very deeply laden, drawing 18 feet with but 5 feet free-
board, and the managing owner, on saying goodbye
off Sandy Hook, warned his skipper to be careful.

After light easterly winds to the Banks, a succession
of fierce westerly gales blew up, so that the *Hendrick
Hudson* had to carry sail to keep the seas astern, and in
four days she covered 800 miles, good work for a packet
in those days. On the evening of the fourth day a big
sea overtook the ship, broke in two of the stern deadlights and poured 6 inches deep through the poop cabin,
at the same time washing away the men from the
wheel. The captain and mate only just got control of
the spinning wheel in time to save a broach to. After
this pooper the skipper took the hint and hove to under
a main spencer.

Gale after gale with only the briefest lulls continued
to hurl the ship along until soundings were reached;
by which time the crew were so worn out that only
15 men out of her complement of 25 were able to go
aloft, and it took all hands including the mate and
the carpenter to reef a topsail. Packet ship fashion,
the royal yards were kept aloft to the last moment, and
it was blowing so hard when the skipper gave orders
for them to be sent down that the main royal yard took
charge and nearly had the man tending the mast rope
aloft overboard. But though the "old man" roared
to him to clear out of it by shinning down the topgallant backstay, he was too good a hand to leave his
job unfinished, and he finally succeeded in securing the
yard and sending it down safely.

With the continual heavy rolling, the new rigging stretched so much that the masts threatened to roll out of her. Preventer backstays were rigged to support the topmasts, whilst the lower shrouds were "cat-harpened" just beneath the futtock shrouds. This class of rigging seamanship is almost an unknown quantity to the present day sailor. The method, however, was quite a simple one; capstan bars were lashed across the shrouds, a tackle rove between port side bar and starboard side bar opposite to it, and sweated up to as near two blocks as strength could get it.

The ship required pumping for a quarter of an hour in each watch. Then, in the heavy rolling, some of the cargo, which was raw turpentine in casks, got stove, and leaking into the hold kept choking the pumps.

Through all this weather the ten cabin passengers, all men, spent their time below under the battened down skylights, playing vingt-et-un, and Leslie declares that the continual "I stand !—double all round !—pay up" ! became terribly monotonous.

Once the ship, during a moonless night when the gale was at its worst, only just missed a barque which was lying hove to under a close-reefed topsail. The sharp cry on deck of "Port ! port ! hard-a-port !" startled the gamblers for a moment, and the game was stopped whilst they listened for the next order. However they quickly resumed when nothing further happened. In those days ships carried no lights, and many were the yarns of unfortunate Bankers run clean over by the hurrying packets.

After strong fair gales all the way across, during which she lost a man overboard and had most of her port bulwarks washed away, the *Hendrick Hudson* was held up by baffling winds in the channel and did not reach London until two days after Christmas.

The return trip to New York was a still worse experience, the little packet taking 70 days from the Downs to Sandy Hook.

Thirteen years later the *Hendrick Hudson*, when westbound with a cargo of rails, foundered in mid-Atlantic, her crew being picked up from the boats by a passing vessel.

The "Montreal's" Cow.

By 1837, the line owned 12 ships, one of which, the *Philadelphia*, built by Christian Bergh in 1832, proudly advertised the possession of a piano. Another, the *Montreal*, of 542 tons and built by Bergh in 1835, had our old friend Delano as her mate; and the equally famous Captain Tinker served as a boy aboard her. Of this ship Tinker used to tell an amusing story. In those days every self-respecting packet carried a cow. *Montreal's* cow dropped out of the slings as she was being hoisted aboard. Falling into the hold she was killed. The *Montreal* sailed, leaving the carcass of the ancient beast behind her. But the sailors of the *Hannibal*, the next packet to leave, complained bitterly of the toughness of the *Montreal's* cow, on which they declared they had been fed the whole way across to London. Tinker remained in the *Montreal* until he obtained command, after which he was shifted into the *Toronto*, of 631 tons, in 1840.   And it was as captain of the *Toronto* that Tinker made his name.

Captain Tinker in the "Toronto" beats the Cunard Steamer.

In the year 1846, he chanced to leave England about the same time as the Cunarder and a new Boston steamer.   On going to say goodbye to a friend, he found him busy writing letters to go by the new Boston boat.   "Give them to me," Tinker is said to have exclaimed; "I'll get them there as soon as she will." The *Toronto* made a fair run across until she found her way blocked by huge fields of broken ice.   Tinker boldly kept her steering to the north, when every other vessel turned south into the baffling variables of the Gulf Stream.   For three days the *Toronto* battled with the ice, but then came her reward.   When Tinker reached New York he found he was the first arrival in six weeks.   The Cunarder had not arrived, the Boston wonder did not reach port for another week.   The daring captain was immediately besieged by newspaper reporters. His *London Times*, 42 days old, was published in a special edition of the *New York Herald* that very afternoon.   His owners pawed him up and down and pounded his chest, "to make certain," as they said, "that he was not a ghost."   Every shipping merchant in South Street came crowding into the Black X office to hear how he had brought the *Toronto* into port; and it was declared on 'Change that if he had put up for President he would have been elected unanimously. Other Black X ships commanded by Tinker were the *Margaret Evans*, 1000 tons, 1864; *Southampton*, 1200 tons, 1847; *Palestine*, 1751 tons, 1856, all three built by Jacob & Westervelt. *Palestine* was his last ship; he left her to take over the London agency for Morgan & Sons, and at the same time acted for Grinnell & Minturn.

The Havre Packets.

Morgan and Grinnell & Minturn were the only two regular packet lines which ran to London, though new lines to Liverpool kept cropping up at intervals, also there were American packets running to Havre as early as 1822. Francis Depaws' was the senior Havre Line, which was afterwards carried on by Fox and Livingston, his sons-in-law

The following were his best known ships in order of date :—

> *Stephania*, Captain John B. Pell,
> *Montano*, Captain Smith,
> *Henry IV.*, Captain William W. Skiddy,
> *Helen Mar*, Captain Harrison,
>   The above were the pioneer ships.
> *Cadmus*, Captain Allyn,
> *Edward Quesnel*, Captain E. Hawkins,
> *Bayard*, Captain Henry Robinson,
> *Howard*, Captain Holdredge,
> *Edward Bonaffe*, Captain James Funk,
> *Queen Mab*, Captain Butman,
> *Don Quixote*, Captain James Clarke.

His sons-in-law added the *Silvie de Grasse*, *Louis Philippe*, *Isaac Bell*, *Havre*, and others.

Captain John Johnston of the "Isaac Bell."

Captain John Johnston of the *Isaac Bell*, who was a master from 1837 to 1854, was wont to declare that in the whole of his sea time he had only known the wind to really blow twice. On one of these occasions, on 16th August, 1839, he was caught by a hurricane when in command of the *Rhone*, and had every stitch of canvas blown off her, until there was not a piece left as large as her captain's hand.

In the *Isaac Bell* Captain Johnston accomplished the remarkable performances of three January passages westward bound, each one in less than 18 days.

The *Rhone* belonged to a second line of Havre packets, amongst whose ships were the *Charles Carroll*, *Erie*, *France*, *Utica*, *Oneida*, *William Tell*, *Baltimore* and *Mercury*.

A third line was started in 1832 by William Whitlock, Junior, with the *Albany*, *Duchesse d'Orleans*, *Formosa*, *Gallia*, *Carolus Magnus*, etc.

The Queer Ways of Captain Bully Hall.

Perhaps the most notorious of all the Havre captains was Captain "Bully" Hall. He had the two 500-ton ships *Superior* and *Splendid* built to his order by Isaac Webb, for the China trade, but in those early days they were too large and glutted the American market with tea and silk, so Captain Hall took the *Splendid* into the Havre trade. Bully Hall, though a very able shipmaster, was a hard nut, with queer ways of administering punishment. He once shut his mate up in the ship's hen-coop and amused himself clucking to him and throwing him corn.

However, he got paid out in his own coin by a little street urchin. The lad happened to be on the dock cooking sweet potatoes in a pitch pot when Bully Hall, in a new fawn-coloured overcoat, came blustering by.

"What have you got there"? he demanded arrogantly of the boy.

"Potatoes, sir."

"What for?"

"To cook 'em, sir."

"Cook this, then," cried Hall, seizing a mop and thrusting it into the pitch pot.

Quick as lightning the boy wiped the mop dripping with pitch on the captain's new overcoat, then ran for his life.

Later New York Packet Lines to Liverpool.

Of the later Liverpool lines, Woodhull & Minturn's was taken over by the Swallow Tail in 1848.

It consisted of four ships:—The *Hottinguer*, Captain Ira Bursley; the *Queen of the West*, Captain Philip Woodhouse, 1168 tons; the *Liverpool*, Captain John Eldridge, 1174 tons (these two ships were built by Brown & Bell in 1843); and the *Constitution*, Captain John Britton, 1400 tons, built in 1848.

This ship and her captain were very well known on the Western Ocean. The *Constitution* was one of the

finest ships of her day and beautifully finished.   Britton
was a most successful shipmaster, and he also gained
renown for his many rescues at sea.   In 1845 he saved
the crew of the ship *Dorchester*, for which he was
presented with a gold medal by the English society
for the preservation of life from shipwreck, and also
testimonials from American sources.

Williams & Guion's Black Star Line.

Then there was Williams & Guion's Black Star
Line.   This firm was partly owned on this side, so that
when sail was outplayed they were able to take up steam
under the English flag.

Their fastest packet was the *Adelaide*, Captain
Robert C. Cutting, which in 1864 ran from New York to
Liverpool in 12 days 8 hours, beating the Cunard
Sidonia, which passed her on her way down New York
Bay.   At least so it was claimed, but Mr. Francis B. C.
Bradlee, who has written a very interesting pamphlet
on the famous *Dreadnought*, quotes from the files of the
New York papers to the effect that the *Adelaide* left on
9th June in company with the Inman Line steamer
Kangaroo, that the *Kangaroo* put back and was delayed
a day or two by engine trouble, and that the two ships
arrived in Liverpool on the same day, 27th June.

As the *Adelaide* was always credited in the shipping
papers with the run of 12 days 8 hours, in which she
beat the *Sidonia*, it is possible that this race with the
Kangaroo was another passage altogether.

Other well-known vessels of the Black Star Line

"ADELAIDE."

Hove to for a Pilot off Sandy Hook.

"JOSHUA BATES."

From the MacPherson Collection.

were the *Guy Mannering*, 1419 tons, built by W. H.
Webb, in 1849, and commanded by Captain Edwards;
the *America*, 1180 tons, built by W. H. Webb and
launched in 1852, her commander being Captain J. J.
Lawrence; and the *Australia*, built by W. H. Webb
and launched 27th July, 1852.

Spofford & Tileston's Patriotic Line.

Spofford & Tileston, who started in 1852 and
rebuilt the old *Henry Clay*, owned the *Orient*, *Webster*,
Calhoun and other ships, most of them built by George
Raynes, of Portsmouth, N.H.

The "Orient," Captain George S. Hill.

The *Orient* was commanded by Captain George S.
Hill, afterwards the secretary of the New York Marine
Society.

In 1856, the *Orient* was chartered by the French
Government to carry wheat to Havre at 25 cents a bushel.
She loaded 80,000 bushels (2100 tons) besides 1000 bags
of flour. Through the stupidity of the French pilot
she was run ashore going into Havre, and whilst being
towed off struck the wall of an old fortification and
broke in two. Somehow Hill managed to save his ship
and patch her up sufficiently to stand the towing across
to Liverpool for repairs; and she continued to make good
money for her owners. She once took 50,000 dollars
freight money in one voyage out and home. This was
capped by the *Webster*, Captain Joseph J. Lawrence,
with a 60,000 dollar voyage.

Robert Kermit's Line to Liverpool.

Robert Kermit also ran some very noted ships to Liverpool, such as the *St. Andrew*, Captain W. C. Thompson, which did the eastward trip in 14 days, the *Virginian*, *Waterloo*, *West Point* and *Constellation*.

The *Waterloo*, under Captain W. H. Allen, was caught in the 18th September gale of 1848 and lost everything on her mainmast above the mainyard. Mr. Kermit used to show pieces of her sails, which had been so knotted up and twisted together by the fury of the wind on this occasion that a marlinspike had no effect upon them.

Allen was one of those captains whom the elements seem to delight in attacking. Whilst master of the *West Point* he found himself in an electric storm, during which his ship was struck six times in one hour and two of his men killed. Again, in 1855, he would have lost the *Constellation* if his passengers had not worked, shift and shift, for days at the pumps.

Boston Packets—The Jewel Line.

The first line of packets started in Boston for the trans-Atlantic service was that of the Boston and Liverpool Packet Company, which commissioned Thatcher Magoun of Medford-on-the-Mystic to build them four ships in 1822.

These were the *Emerald*, *Amethyst*, *Topaz* and *Sapphire*. The firm were evidently not very experienced and engaged a separate agent in Liverpool for each ship, but this curious plan did not succeed and the enterprise failed in 1827.   Nevertheless they were smart little ships and well officered.

Extraordinary Eastward Passage of the "Emerald."

The *Emerald*, with a tonnage of 359 tons, length of 110 feet and beam of 27 feet, was loftily rigged, crossing skysail yards.   In 1824, under Captain Philip Fox of Cohasset, she made the astonishing passage of 17 days from Liverpool to Boston.

At 3 p.m. on 20th February, she left the Mersey, picked up an easterly gale and carried it all the way to the Boston Light, where she hove to for a pilot at 3 p.m. on 8th March.   Captain Fox had kept her travelling with all the sail she would bear, and her lee rail was under water most of the time.   When she anchored off Fort Independence three hours later, her owners thought she had put back in trouble, but their concern was changed into jubilance when Captain Fox calmly handed them the Liverpool papers of 20th February.

This wonderful passage was undoubtedly due more to the hard driving of Captain Fox and the lucky easterly slant than to any unusual speed in the *Emerald*.   Fox was a noted carrier of sail, and it was not the first time that he had forced a ship beyond her designed speed.

The "Topaz" captured by Pirates.

Interest attaches to the little *Topaz* for a very different reason.   Soon after the firm had failed, the *Topaz* went a Calcutta voyage under Captain Brewster. On her homeward passage she was captured by pirates when close to St. Helena and her whole ship's company butchered. The pirate was a Spanish brig called the *Macrinarian*, Captain Mansel Alcantra, and the date was 1829. About the same time he took the *Caudace* of Marblehead, whose supercargo escaped by dressing up as a priest. The Spaniards, whether pirates or otherwise, are always extremely devout, and when they came upon the supposed priest telling his beads in the cabin they crossed themselves and hurriedly decamped.

There were several pirates preying upon "flying fish sailors" in the Southern Seas about that time. The best known of these was Benito de Soto of the *Black Joke*, who plundered the *Morning Star* in 1832.

Another slim schooner was the terror of the Indian Ocean, and was known amongst the Indiamen as the "Black Pirate." He usually lurked under the high land of Madagascar, and with the aid of sweeps pounced out on becalmed East Indiamen and "Country" ships. He caught a tartar at last in the shape of a trooper in charge of a naval officer, and was fought off and left in a sinking condition.

The Second Line of Boston Packets.

Owing to the enterprise of Henry Hall, Joshua Blake, David Henshaw and other Bostonians, a second line of packets was started in 1827. Its first ship, the *Dover*, of 425 tons, was built at Charlestown by John M. Robertson and commanded by the well-known Captain Ira Bursley. The fare asked to Liverpool was 140 dollars including bedding and wine.

According to her plan of accommodation, the *Dover* had a main cabin 45 feet long, with eleven 6 feet state-rooms opening into it, the head room in which was 7 feet. She had what was then called a bathing room on deck—there were no fitted baths, of course, a good sluice with cold water out of a bucket being considered quite good enough in those robust days. A library is shown, but there is no mention of a smoking room.

The other ships of the line were all built by Thatcher Magoun; 500 tonners named the *New England, Lowell, Trenton, Plymouth, Boston*, and *Liverpool*.

This line also failed to succeed and only lasted about half-a-dozen years. The trouble in those early days was that Boston could not provide anything more valuable for export than what were called "notions," such as rubber shoes, cow horns and corn husks, and the outward packets were forced to go to Charleston, South Carolina, for a cargo of cotton. This was the real cause why neither of these two pioneer lines was a success.

Enoch Train's White Diamond Line.

The most important line of Boston packets was that of Enoch Train, one of the most enterprising of the shipowners and merchants in the United States during the first half of the nineteenth century. This he inaugurated in 1843. He already was trading to South America with the ships *Dorchester, Cairo* and *Governor Davis* in the thirties, when he decided to enter the Baltic trade with a vessel of much greater size than any previously used in that trade.   This project resulted in the famous *St. Petersburg*, built by Waterman & Ewell of Medford in 1839.   This ship was in all respects a packet ship with square stern, painted ports, and large accommodation for passengers.   Of 814 tons burthen she measured 160 feet by 33.

When she descended upon the Baltic cotton trade in charge of that dandy skipper, Richard Trask, she created a sensation at every port she touched at.

Trask was one of those princely owner-skippers with the grand manner.   Wherever he went he entertained largely, and it is even stated that as soon as he had arranged at St. Petersburg for his return cargo he would leave the ship in charge of his first officer and return *via* London by steamer.

When Enoch Train decided to run packets from Boston to Liverpool, he diverted the four ships to the Atlantic whilst his new packets were building.   As already mentioned the captain and crew of the *Dorchester* were rescued from the sinking ship on 6th December, 1845, by Captain John Britton; but by this date the first of Enoch Train's new packets was already on the Western Ocean.

Enoch Train and Donald McKay.

Americans always speak of Donald McKay as the greatest genius in the history of their shipbuilding trade.   Not only was he a master builder, but as a designer he had such vision that he was always well in advance of the times: he broke the way and others tried their best to follow.   And the man who really gave him his chance was Enoch Train.

Donald McKay claimed descent from the Highland chieftain who died as far back as 1395.   He was born at Shelburne, Nova Scotia, in 1810, and with his brother, Lauchlan, had built a fishing boat when he should have been at school.

He was no more than sixteen years of age when he went to New York, and started to learn his trade in the shipyard of Isaac Webb on the East River.   At the age of thirty he was an acknowledged master of his profession, and was accepted as such by John Currier, junior, of Newburyport, who took him into partnership in 1841.

The first ship which had the McKay imprint upon it was the *Delia Walker*, launched in Currier's yard in 1840. Her owner, Dennis Coudry, during his many visits to the ship on the stocks was so impressed by McKay's all round ability, that when in 1843 he met Enoch Train whilst crossing the Atlantic in a Cunarder he could not resist sounding the praises of the young shipbuilder.   Enoch Train was crossing in order to establish European agencies for his projected line; and as a result of his conversation with Coudry decided to see Donald McKay on his return, with a view to the building of his pioneer ship.

Meanwhile Currier and McKay had built the barque *Mary Broughton* in 1841, and the ships *Courier* and *Ashburton* in 1842, the *Courier* having the honour of being the first ship designed by McKay.

At this point Captain Clark records that the firm went into dissolution, "the models and moulds being equally divided—with a saw."

But the little *Courier* of 380 tons was already out-sailing everything in the Rio coffee trade and making the name of her designer.

Donald McKay now joined in partnership with Pickett at Newburyport, and in 1843 built the packet ship, *St. George*, 845 tons, the pioneer ship of the Red Cross Line.

When Enoch Train and Donald McKay met at Newburyport, on Train's return from Europe, "it was the swift contact of flint and steel," in Captain Clark's enthusiastic words, and the contract for the *Joshua Bates*, the pioneer ship of the white Diamond Line, was signed within an hour.

On the day that this ship was launched, Enoch Train's enthusiasm once more caught fire, and he urged Donald McKay to give up Newburyport and come to Boston; with the clinching argument that his financial backing would be behind the builder.

And thus it was that McKay, at 34 years of age, was able to open his yard at the foot of Border Street, East Boston, where he launched one triumph of the shipbuilder's art after another.

In the Appendix I give a list of the chief ships built by Donald McKay from his own designs. Between 1845 and 1850, he built the following ships for Enoch Train:—*Washington Irving, Anglo-Saxon, Ocean Monarch, Anglo-American* and *Daniel Webster*.

McKay's packet ships were celebrated for their strength; they were designed to carry a tremendous press of sail in heavy weather without straining. In light winds, they were not fast, but then packet ships did not sail in the latitudes of light winds.

McKay's "Daniel Webster."

McKay's *Daniel Webster* will serve as a good example of a first class packet in the fifties.

She came out in 1851, measured 1500 tons burthen, 1187 tons register, 186 feet length from head to taffrail, 40 feet beam, 24 feet depth of hold, and a draught of 16 feet. Under water she was as sharp as a wedge, though full enough above with ample bearings. She was a three decker, with a poop extending to the main hatch, connecting with almost as long a topgallant foc's'le by gangway ladders, so that the ship could be worked without a man having to put step on the main deck.

The following particulars, showing the strength of her build, may perhaps interest old seamen. Her keel of rock maple was 32 inches deep by 4 wide. Over this were three keelsons, each 15 inches square, bolted through and through with bolts, alternately copper and iron, each $1\frac{1}{4}$ inches in diameter. She had two sister keelsons 15 inches square, and her bilge keels were of heavier dimensions. Her apron, stem and stern post, indeed, her whole frame, was of white oak. Forward she had seven breasthooks and "pointers" of huge dimensions. Her timbers were placed as close as possible: the garboard strake 7 inches thick and proportionately strong to the wales. The ceiling of yellow pine was 4 inches, increasing to the lower deck clamps, where it was 8 inches thick. In the lower hold 7 beams ran athwartship, which were all kneed off above and below. The deck beams, of southern pine, were 16 inches by 12, 6 feet apart, and plentifully interspersed with carlings of great strength.

She was fitted with many new improvements, including Robinson's patent steering apparatus, and hydraulic pumps so constructed that they could be worked under any circumstances and could never become choked. And if strength was the first thought in her construction it was not allowed to spoil her looks, and we are told that "wherever there was anything that would have appeared unsightly or heavy it was relieved by bold carving, touched with gold."

Her figure-head was naturally the great American statesman, holding in his right hand the Articles of the Constitution; her trail-boards were richly carved, as was her stern, which showed the American Eagle and British Lion; whilst the saloon under the poop was "fitted elegantly in rich deep-veined mahogany, with columns relieved with gold, and ceiling of white and gold."

Her accommodation was unusually good. She had a second-class saloon, ice-house, two hospitals and a surgeon's laboratory. On the lower deck, which was fitted with iron berths, she had accommodation for 450 persons, whilst below this the timbering was prepared for another deck should it ever be required.

The *Daniel Webster*, though only an 11-knot ship, passed Cape Clear on her maiden passage 13 days 10 hours from Boston. Beating to windward in a hard wind showed her at her best; indeed this might be said to be the case with all the packets. Owing to the beautiful flat set of their cotton canvas, and the sharpness with which their yards could be braced up, they could generally head a point higher than other ships. A case in proof was the race up Channel between the beautiful iron clipper *Baron Colonsay* and the Swallow Tail packet *E. W. Stetson*.

Weatherliness of the Packets—Race between "E. W. Stetson" and the Iron Clipper "Baron Colonsay."

It was a dead beat up, and though the *Baron Colonsay* went through the water about 3 knots an hour faster than the *Stetson*, the Yankee could head a point or more higher, with the result that, after a tussle of several days' duration, they took their pilots together. This speaks well for the *Stetson*, for a writer in the "Nautical" states that in 1880 he personally knew the *Baron Colonsay* to average 15 knots for 24 hours. "She took out all our logline, which was measured to 17 knots —and myself nearly with it as I was heaving the log— moreover, our sights on the two consecutive days corroborate the distance we had estimated as having run. This was with the commencement of a gale, whilst the sea was comparatively smooth. After about 30 hours of it we had to shorten down, but could then run comfortably 13 knots for days together."

The *E. W. Stetson* was not built for a packet, and resembled more the later Down East Cape Horners, and was what Americans would call a medium clipper. With regard to the weatherliness of the packets, Mr. Leslie (speaking of the early Black X liners) writes, "Old Channel pilots, after having been in charge of one of these little packets, used to tell marvellous tales about their handiness, and how they could turn them to windward through passages like the Gull Stream on their way to the Downs or through the Needles Channel as easily as one of their own pilot boats."

No one ever saw an American ship with her sails set carelessly, and everything aloft was always of the best in order to stand the tremendous carrying on indulged in by American officers.

All the leech lines and bunt lines were also spilling lines on American ships, so that the sails could be snugged up to the yards, even when it was blowing hard. Thus it was no uncommon sight to see a packet carrying main royal with wind abeam and passing ships under close-reefed topsails and foresail.

An instance of this was given me by Captain Paton, who sailed the *E. W. Stetson* for some years.

"Once when off Portland Bill, a fresh W.S.W. wind blowing, I could see about a dozen ships and barques away to windward, some more than hull down. At that time we were carrying main royal and the other ships were beginning to shorten sail. At 9 p.m. I tacked to the southward with Portland lights right astern. During the night we tacked three times, and at 8 a.m. were standing in for the Start, the lighthouse well on the starboard bow. Although it was blowing quite strong we were still carrying our main royal; and the fishermen, as we passed them, stood up and gave us three cheers. All those ships which had been so much to windward the evening before were now hull down to leeward and under close-reefed topsails (one of these same ships was the *Hudson*, belonging to Morgan's Black X Line, which had left the docks a few days before us). When we got within a mile of the land near Prawle Point the wind suddenly shifted to N.N.E., and all we had to do was trim sail and set a course down Channel. All the other ships had to make sail, so we left them out of sight astern very quickly. That time we did a quick passage to New York, viz., 27 days from London. I have always been proud of that beat from Portland to Prawle Point in 12 hours. I do not think the China clippers could have done any better, for it was a dead beat to windward, the wind being steady W.S.W. all night."

The *E. W. Stetson* was still in Lloyd's Register as late as 1905. She registered 1141 tons; was built at Damariscotta in 1862; was 173.2 feet long, 38.2 feet beam, and 23.6 feet depth. In her old age she was bought by the Tice Towing Company of New York, turned into a barge, and only disappeared about 12 years ago, when she broke adrift from her tug and drove ashore.

Later Ships of Enoch Train's.

Enoch Train's Line of Boston Packets developed very rapidly; and from an old poster of the early fifties I find the following ships in his sailing list:—*North America, George Raynes, Daniel Webster, Moses Wheeler, Parliament, Levi Woodbury, President, Plymouth Rock, Sunbeam, North Atlantic, Anglo-American, Ben Rock, George Washington, Cromwell, William Wirt, Clara Wheeler, Revere, Washington Irving, Western Star, Rose Standish, Napoleon, Faneuil Hall, Old England* and *Staffordshire*—a fleet of 24 packets, advertised to sail from Boston semi-monthly and from Liverpool every week.

"Staffordshire"—the Clipper of the White Diamond Fleet.

In the centre of this poster there is a fine representation of the *Staffordshire*, with a prominent T showing just below the close-reef band of her fore topsail.

The *Staffordshire* was built by Donald McKay in 1851, and was a good deal sharper and finer lined than was usual with packet ships.

Her figure-head was a finely carved bust of a witch. Her stern was also elaborately decorated with carving, being ornamented on one side with a manufacturing scene from Staffordshire and on the other with a model of the building on Lewis wharf, which was Enoch Train's place of business.

Commanded by Albert H. Brown, the *Staffordshire*

"DANIEL WEBSTER."

" RACER."

in 1851 made a run from Boston to Liverpool of 13½ days, pilot to pilot, or 14 days 18 hours from dock to dock.

With the Californian gold excitement at its height, Enoch Train decided to send his clipper round the Horn in 1852. For this ocean race he required a racing skipper, and he was lucky in being able to engage Captain Josiah Richardson, who, in the previous year, had driven the extreme McKay clipper *Staghound* from New York to 'Frisco in 107 days, in spite of the loss of her main topmast and three topgallant masts, which compelled Richardson to put into Valparaiso for repairs when only 66 days out.

The *Staffordshire* was specially rigged and fitted for this voyage, and sailed from Boston on 3rd May. Her outward passage was one of the best of the year.

She crossed the Equator 25 days out; passed Cape San Roque 3 days later; from San Roque to 50° S. took 25 days; rounded the Horn from 50° S. to 50° S. in 14 days, crossing the parallel of 50° S. in the Pacific on 8th July; crossed the Equator in 110° W. on 24th July, 16 days only from 50° S. (According to Maury this run from 50° S. to the Equator appears to be the record, the next best being *Flying Cloud's* 17 days in August, 1851.)

From the Equator to the Golden Gate, *Staffordshire* also made an excellent run of 18 days, arriving San Francisco on 13th August, 101 days out from her Boston pilot.

The clipper ship *Shooting Star*, which had sailed

from Boston about the same time as the *Staffordshire*, arrived in 'Frisco Bay on 17th August, four days later. Unfortunately I have been unable to obtain any particulars of *Staffordshire's* homeward passage, but it was equally good and is given by American authorities as only 82 days from 'Frisco to Boston.

After this very successful venture amongst the Cape Horn flyers, the *Staffordshire*, still commanded by Captain Richardson, returned to the Atlantic.

The Wreck of the "Staffordshire."

On 30th December, 1854, when bound from Liverpool to Boston, the gallant ship came to a tragic end, striking on the Blonde Rock, Cape Sable, during a thick fog. Two days before Captain Richardson had had a severe fall on the deck and injured his spine. The ship struck whilst he was lying helpless in his bunk. Whilst he lay suffering in an agony of suspense, Joseph Alden, the chief officer, came in and reported that the ship had slipped off the rock into deep water and was foundering.

Captain Richardson gave his orders for the saving of the women and children, but refused himself to leave his ship, his last words being:—"God's will be done."

The last scenes of the disaster were agonising. There was far from room for all the emigrants in the boats, and only 44 souls were saved out of 214. In Boston the story went that hatchets were freely used and clinging fingers cut off in the fierce struggle to prevent the people in the water from swamping the overloaded boats in their efforts to save themselves.

Train's Line suffered an equally terrible disaster in the burning of the *Ocean Monarch*, with the loss of 400 lives, when leaving Liverpool in August, 1848.

The news of this tragedy was brought to Boston by the ss. *Persia*, Captain Judkins. Hundreds of people were waiting to see the *Persia* dock and gather the latest news from Europe. As the ship was passing her lines, Captain Judkins shouted the story of the *Ocean Monarch* across the narrowing strip of water, and the heart-rending scene that then took place on the dockside was never forgotten by those who witnessed it.

"Star of Empire" and "Chariot of Flame."

In 1853 Donald McKay built the big sister ships, *Star of Empire* and *Chariot of Fame*, of 2050 tons American measurement, for the White Diamond Line.

The romantic names of many of the McKay built clippers are worthy of notice—these have been attributed to their designer, who was peculiarly happy in his choice of fitting titles. Mr. S. E. Morison, in his standard work on the *Maritime History of Massachusetts*, pays a fine tribute to Donald McKay's character, which I cannot resist quoting:—"Donald McKay was an unusual combination of artist and scientist, of idealist and practical man of business. With dark hair, curling back from a high intellectual forehead, powerful Roman nose, inscrutable brown eyes, and firm lips, he was as fair to look upon as his ships. His serene and beautiful character won him the respect and affection of his employees, and made the atmosphere of his shipbuilding yard that of a happy, loyal family. . . . Experience, character, and mathematics self-taught, were the firm soil from which the genius of Donald McKay blossomed. He designed every vessel built in his yard, and personally attended to every detail of her construction. . . When the great frames were in place, Donald McKay would inspect the ship's skeleton from every angle, clothing it in imagination with skin of oak: and if any thing looked wrong by perhaps an eighth of an inch he chalked a frame for shaving off or filling out. "

The *Chariot of Fame* was always said to have been Enoch Train's special favourite of all his many packets. She was given one or two special luxuries, such as a reading room on the quarter-deck for her cabin passengers. Captain Knowles was her first commander. When Enoch Train was brought down in the American financial crash of 1857, the *Chariot of Fame* was sold to the Liverpool White Star Line, and carried many thousands of emigrants to Australia and New Zealand, her best run to Melbourne being 66 days from the Tuskar. She came to her end in January, 1876, being abandoned when bound from the Chincha Islands to Cork.

The Red Cross Line.

The Red Cross Line, or the St. George's Cross Line as it was usually advertised on this side of the Atlantic, is chiefly remembered for one ship, the famous packet *Dreadnought*.   Yet the pioneer ship which gave its name to the line was built ten years before the *Dreadnought*.

This was the *St. George* of 845 tons, already mentioned as being built by Donald McKay & Pickett at Newburyport in 1843.   Then came the *St. Patrick* of 906 tons, which was followed by the *Andrew Foster*, *Driver*, *Racer*, *Highflyer*, and *Dreadnought*, all built at Newburyport.

The line was promoted by some very well-known New York financiers, amongst whom were Governor E. D. Morgan, Francis B. Cutting and David Ogden.

None of their ships lasted very long except the *Dreadnought*.   The *St. Patrick* was wrecked 2 miles south of Barnegat on 19th December, 1854; the *Andrew Foster* had a still shorter life, being run into and sunk in the Irish Channel.   The *Driver*, which was a fast ship and once made the difficult west-bound passage in 19 days, was posted missing with 600 souls on board; the *Racer*, the clipper of the fleet before the advent of the *Dreadnought*, was lost after a few passages, on the Blackwater Bank in the Irish Channel, whilst the *Highflyer*, which was built the same year as the *Dreadnought*, was sent out to 'Frisco in 1855, and whilst crossing the Pacific to Hongkong disappeared and was never heard of again.

The "Racer"—Spar Measurements and Sail Area.

Before we proceed to consider the *Dreadnought* and her records, the following details of the *Racer* will give a good idea of the previous ships of the St. George's Cross Line.

She cost £25,000 to build, registered 1696 tons, with a length on the keel of 200 feet, length on deck 207 feet, beam 42 feet 6 inches and depth of 28 feet. Her dead rise at half floor was 10 inches, and her loaded draught was 20 feet. She was a three decker, with large loading ports, one on each side in the upper 'tween decks, and two on each side in the lower 'tween decks. Between the fore and main masts she had a large house, 47 feet by 18, in which were the crew and passenger galleys, the hospital, boys' room, vegetable house and ice house.

Her figure-head was the finely carved and gilded head of a racehorse, whilst her stern was ornamented with a large spread eagle, a very favourite subject for the ornamentation under the taffrail of ships flying the Stars and Stripes, though I do not think any set heraldic design was ever the rule.

The following measurements will give a good idea of her sail plan :—

Foremast	84 feet long	31 inches diameter
Fore topmast	47 ,, ,,	17 ,, ,,
Fore topgallant mast	26 ,, ,,	11 ,, ,,
Fore royal mast	16 ,, ,,	9 ,, ,,
Freoyard	47 ,, ,,	
Fore topsail yard	60 ,, ,,	
Fore topgallant yard	44 ,, ,,	
Fore royal yard	34 ,, ,,	
Bowsprit	30 feet outboard	
Jibboom and flying jibboom	33 ,,	
Sail area (about)	8152 square yards	

Captain Samuel Samuels.

In the days of wood and hemp, the captains of celebrated ships held their place amongst the noted men of the world. They ranked with other great leaders of men, as the heads of a great profession—that of the sea. Their names were as familiar to the man in the street as those of great politicians, great admirals or great generals. Alas! that steel and steam have changed all this. Ships still figure largely in the press when notorious for size or speed, but their captains scarcely ever. They have ceased to be public men, in spite of the fact that their importance to the world is even greater than it used to be.

But in the fifties and sixties the civilised world turned over in its bed and suddenly took a notion (as it has done more than once in its history) to spread itself. The old nations swarmed into their ships and set sail for the new unexplored parts of the world, which, through this eager influx of stout hearts, have in their turn become nations. Perhaps this general "going afloat" explains the world-wide notoriety of the great sea captains of that era. As regards this notoriety one may say that what Toynbee was to the Blackwall frigates and Anthony Enright to the Australian Black Ballers, that Captain Samuels of the *Dreadnought* was to the Yankee packets. Both he and his ship have been written about and sung about times and again. Samuels owned a fine oil painting of the *Dreadnought* by Walters; the public demand for the celebrated ship's picture was so great that the stone of the lithograph was completely worn out by the number of prints required.

This famous packet captain was a man of unusually marked individuality. Iron determination and a total lack of fear predominated, but those useful gifts, great executive ability, and attention to detail, no doubt contributed in no small degree to his success.

When he took hold, one could consider the matter done with, for he was one of those who rarely failed, however difficult the task. He spared neither himself nor his ship nor his men; indeed, I fear he was a hard taskmaster even for the Atlantic.

There is an old sailor still alive in Sussex whose proudest boast is that he made a voyage on the *Dreadnought*. He bears the true hall-mark of the packet-rat over his eyes, in the shape of scars and dents made by knuckle dusters: and he has some grim yarns of Samuels as a sail carrier and a man driver. This man's brother was the *Dreadnought's* bosun and man-handler for seven years; and he declares that the "working up of their old irons" began as a rule before the ship was outside the pierhead. He also has a story that Samuels once shot three men on the foreyard, two of whom died, and that for this bit of gun play the captain did twelve months in prison. After making inquiries, I have not been able to confirm this episode: no doubt the years have coloured it. But one thing is certain—that Samuels was not a man to be trifled with. Indeed his own virile narrative of the taming of the "Bloody Forty" is a sufficient proof of this. In appearance he was just what one would expect of such a character. Standing about 5 ft. 10 ins. of powerful frame and splendid physique, he looked the hard customer that he was.

In his book *From Forecastle to Cabin* he has told of his adventurous early years. Naturally such a boy would run away to sea. Samuels fled from home at the age of eleven, and shipped as cabin boy on a coasting schooner, the *Hampton Westcott*. His next ship was the schooner *Rio*. He left her to serve as a seaman on the Revenue brig *Jefferson*. After a short experience on the *Jefferson*, he found himself shanghaied aboard the Baltimore ship *Belvedere*, which took him to Liverpool. Here he shipped on the Liverpool ship *Emily*. He ran from her in Galveston, and signed on the Texas frigate *Houston*, only to desert in New Orleans, where for a short time his sea life was interrupted whilst he fancied himself on the boards as a vaudeville singer. Luckily this sideslip was righted by another shanghai-ing, this time on the ship *Ocmulgee*, bound for Liverpool. From Liverpool he sailed as seaman of the ship *Chester* to Philadelphia. In Philadelphia he shipped before the mast in the *St. Lawrence* for a round voyage. She was his first "Sou-Spainer," and gave him his fill of adventure, including ghosts, cannibals and a spill overboard. After this he returned to the Atlantic and became second mate of the *Henry Pratt*, then mate of the British ship *Caledonia*, which he left owing to his ideas of discipline being too severe for the Red Ensign. Though a boy in years, he was now a man in experience, and proved his worth as

mate of the following ships across the Western Ocean:—
Leander, *Metoka*, *Rockall*, *Vicksburg*, *Wabash*, *Jessore*,
Independence, *Manhattan*, and the Dutch ship *Angelique*,
of which last he became master at the age of twenty-one.

Here his success was so great that the owners of the
Red Cross Line determined to build a ship specially
for him. The result was the *Dreadnought*. Her keel
was laid in June, 1853, at Newburyport on the Merrimac.
Samuels himself overlooked every detail of her construction, and it is characteristic of him that he sent
over to England specially to get the correct spelling of
her name, which there is no doubt he chose himself.

The *Dreadnought* was launched on 6th October, and
measured 1400 tons, 200 feet long, by 40.25 feet
beam, and 26 feet depth of hold. Her mean loaded
draught was 21 to 22 feet, and her mainyard was 79 feet
long.

The "Dreadnought" called "The Wild Boat of the Atlantic."

The *Dreadnought* was not an extreme clipper in
point of design, but was given a large spread of canvas.
The great aim in building her was to produce a vessel
with the power and strength to carry a heavy press of
sail in the strongest wind, and this aim was most
successfully attained. Here is Samuels' own testimony:
"She possessed the merit of being able to bear driving
as long as her sails and spars would stand." Yet, in
spite of this merit, there is no doubt that her captain
had more to do with her quick passages than her designer,

CAPTAIN SAMUEL SAMUELS.

By courtesy of the "Nautical Magazine."

" DREADNOUGHT. "

From a Drawing in possession of the Author

for in light winds she was slow and it is doubtful whether she was really much more than an 11-knot ship; it certainly required a gale of wind to show her at her best. On such occasions she was an extraordinary ship. "Many a time," says Captain Samuels, "I have been told that the crews of other vessels, lying hove to, could see our keel, as we jumped from sea to sea under every rag we could carry." No wonder that she was called the "Flying Dutchman" and "The Wild Boat of the Atlantic."

Possibly some of my readers may be inclined to dispute my statement that the *Dreadnought* was not a fast ship in ordinary winds. Here Captain Paton's testimony may be of value. He wrote to me some years ago as follows:—"I have seen the *Dreadnought*: was in company with her at sea once : she did very little with the *E. W. Stetson*, and as the latter was not at all fast, the former could not have been so. However, like a good many Boston ships, no doubt she did well in very strong winds, but in moderate weather the British tea clippers—(note: Captain Paton served his time in the tea clipper, *Flying Spur*)—would have left her out of sight in a very short time."

This is all very well, but a few pages back we had an instance of what the *E. W. Stetson* could do with the fast iron clipper *Baron Colonsay*—and I doubt if this story of her success over a fellow packet will help to prove Captain Paton's contention that the *E. W. Stetson* was a slow ship.

One year the *E. W. Stetson* and *Isaac Webb* were

loading in the East River, New York.   Whilst yarning
in the *Stetson's* cabin, Captain Urquhart of the *Isaac
Webb* began cracking up his own ship to Captain Paton,
who was then mate of the *Stetson* under Captain Moore,
and declared that the *Isaac Webb* could easily do over
12 knots.   He then enquired how the *Stetson* sailed.
Captain Paton replied that she sailed very badly, and
when making 10 knots (her speed limit) there was
white water for about a mile all round.

The *Isaac Webb* sailed for Liverpool about four days
before the *E. W. Stetson* cleared for London.   When
making sail outside Sandy Hook, those on the *Stetson*
saw the *Isaac Webb* right ahead about six miles off.
The wind was moderate at north, and as soon as all sail
was on her, the *Stetson* began to come up on the *Isaac
Webb* hand over fist.   The former was steered to pass
the *Isaac Webb* to leeward and close to.   And as they
went by, Captain Urquhart and his wife were leaning
over the quarter of the *Isaac Webb*, watching the
Stetson with amazement in their faces.   Just as the
ships were alongside each other, with the *Stetson* forging
rapidly ahead, Captain Urquhart called out:—"I
thought you said that ship could not sail."

Quick as a flash came back Paton's retort:—"You
are the first ship we have ever passed."   With a look
of disgust and a shake of his fist, Captain Urquhart
turned away, and no doubt there was some slight
unpleasantness aboard the *Isaac Webb* for a few moments.

To return to the "Wild Boat of the Atlantic."   Her
best 24 hours run was 387 knots, coming east, I believe,

though I would not be certain. It was at night that Samuels drove her hardest. He had a shelf built in his after-companionway on which he was accustomed to lie down during the night. It was purposely made too short to allow him to stretch out and sleep comfortably, thus he always had his weather-eye open and the least change in the wind or work on deck brought him out at once.

The *Dreadnought* had been originally intended for the "Racehorse Line" to California; but the loss of six of their ships in succession and the high rates to Liverpool were the cause of her joining the Atlantic packets. On her first voyage, she made the round trip in 58 days and cleared a profit of 40,000 dollars. Her outward cargo consisted of 3827 barrels of flour, 24,150 bushels of wheat, 12,750 bushels of corn, 304 bales of cotton, 198 barrels of potash, 150 boxes of bacon, and 5600 staves, which with 60 tons of ballast made a total deadweight of 1559.65 tons.

The passage to Liverpool, in December, 1853, took 24 days. But the return passage made her reputation. She sailed in February, the day after the Cunard steamer, *Canada*, and reported off the Highlands of New Jersey, 19 days out, on the same day that the *Canada* reached Boston.

From that date Samuels guaranteed to make deliveries within a specified time or forfeit freight charges. In this way the *Dreadnought* gained freight rates midway between those of the steamers and other sailing packets.

It was also on her maiden voyage that she gained the

distinction of being the first full rigged ship to pass through Hell Gate at night.

On her second voyage *Dreadnought* made the following times:

From New York arrived Liverpool, April, 1854—18 days out.

From Liverpool arrived New York, June, 1854—26 days out.

On her third voyage—

From New York arrived Liverpool, August, 1854—30 days out.

From Liverpool arrived New York, October, 1854—29 days out.

It was on her fourth voyage that she first made a passage which came within the 14 days—Captain Clark has given the runs of the *Dreadnought's* best passages and I take the liberty of transcribing them.

NEW YORK TO LIVERPOOL.

Nov.	20.—Passed Sandy Hook at 6.30 p.m.				
,,	21.—Distance run, 120 miles.				
,,	22.—	,,	,,	57	,,
,,	23.—	,,	,,	225	,,
,,	24.—	,,	,,	300	,,
,,	25.—	,,	,,	175	,,
,,	26.—	,,	,,	125	,,
,,	27.—	,,	,,	250	,,
,,	28.—	,,	,,	263	,,
,,	29.—	,,	,,	240	,,
,,	30.—	,,	,,	270	,,
Dec.	1.—	,,	,,	242	,,
,,	2.—	,,	,,	222	,, Off Cape Clear.
,,	3.—	,,	,,	212	,,
,,	4.—	,,	,,	320	,,

At noon took her pilot off Point Lynas, had to wait 8 hours for water on the bar, anchored in the Mersey

10 p.m. The actual time in covering 3071 miles was 14 days 4 hours; allowing for the 8 hours wait off the bar and difference of longitude, this gives a passage of 13 days 11 hours.

On 20th May, 1855, *Dreadnought* arrived at Liverpool in 15 days 12 hours.

In 1856 she made two very good east-bound passages: —the first in January when she made a 24-hour run of 312 miles, averaged 222 miles a day, and arrived Liverpool on 9th February, out 14 days 8 hours; the second in May when she covered the distance in 16 days.

In 1857 *Dreadnought's* best passage was on the more difficult west-bound run, when she arrived New York in February, 21 days out, but it is stated from responsible quarters that she was only 15 days from land to land.

In 1859 she made the best passage of her career according to Captain Samuels.

On Feb. 27.—At 3 p.m. she discharged her New York pilot.

On Feb. 28.—Distance run 200 miles. Wind South to W.N.W., brisk breezes.

On March 1.—Distance run, 293 miles. Wind W.N.W., fresh breeze.

On March 2.—Distance run, 262 miles. Brisk gales and snow squalls from N.W. to N.N.W.

On March 3.—Distance run 208 miles. Heavy gales and snow squalls, N.N.W. to North.

On March 4.—Distance run 178 miles. Heavy gales and snow squalls, N.N.E. to North.

On March 5.—Distance run 218 miles. Heavy gales and snow squalls, North to N.N.E.

On March 6.—Distance run, 133 miles. Wind N.E. to South, light.

On March 7.—Distance run, 282 miles. Wind S.S.E., brisk breeze and clear.

On March 8.—Distance run, 313 miles. S.S.W. to South, fresh breeze and clear.

On March 9.—Distance run, 268 miles. Brisk gales, South to S.E.

On March 10.—Distance run, 205 miles. Wind S.E. to S.W., brisk breeze and squally.

On March 11.—Distance run, 308 miles. Wind South to S.W. strong breeze and squally.

On March 12.—Distance run, 150 miles. Wind S.W., thick weather.

Distance from Sandy Hook to North-West Lightship, 3018 miles.

It is on this passage that a controversy has raged over a statement made by Captain Samuels in his old age, that at the end of 9 days 17 hours the *Dreadnought* was off Queenstown and sent her mails ashore by a Cork pilot-boat.

A 9-day passage between Sandy Hook and Queenstown is quite within the possibilities of a ship like the *Dreadnought.*

The owners of the *Guy Mannering* claimed two 9-day passages to Cape Clear for that ship, and it is also claimed that the *N. B. Palmer* crossed from Sandy Hook to the Lizard in 9 days.

It certainly does not seem possible that the *Dreadnought* was anywhere near Queenstown on the 10th day of this passage.   Her time from Sandy Hook to the North-West Lightship is given as 13 days 8 hours mean time, by Captain Clark.   She arrived in Liverpool an hour later.

But in June of the same year according to notices in the *New York Herald* and *Illustrated London News* she was very near Captain Samuels' 9 days 17 hours.

She was reported as passing Sandy Hook on 16th June at 12.30 p.m. by the *New York Herald*, and as off Cape Clear on 27th June, 9 days from New York by the

Illustrated London News. It was then probably that the wind became variable and died down, as Captain Samuels declared, referring by mistake to the previous eastward passage, for the *Dreadnought* did not reach Liverpool till 2nd July. Captain Samuels may easily have been held up off Sandy Hook and not taken his departure for some hours or even a couple of days after he was reported from Sandy Hook, and he would undoubtedly have reckoned his 9 days 7 hours from the log entry time of his departure, so that it seems to me that this record claimed by so many for the *Dreadnought* must belong to this passage—and that Captain Samuels in his old age mixed the two passages up.

The only satisfactory way of being sure of actual times in passages of sailing ships is from the ships' official log books or from the abstracts kept by one or other of their officers.

I do not think it greatly matters whether the *Dreadnought* was 9 days 17 hours or 10 days 17 hours or more or less, the fact remains that, given the wind, she was capable of breaking the record and certainly had by far the best average of any of the packets.

In the Appendix I have collected a number of fast Atlantic passages claimed for packets as well as clippers and even yachts, but there are so many different ways by which captains reckon passages that where no details are given one must allow a margin of even a couple of days—though most passages, when no details are given, are supposed to be reckoned from departure to pilot.

In July, 1859, the struggle between Captain Samuels and the "Bloody Forty" took place on the return passage to New York. The details of this attempted mutiny I give later on from the captain's own words.

In the year 1862, during a passage to the westward, Samuels had the most unpleasant experience of his life and the famous *Dreadnought* the extraordinary indignity of being sailed backwards for some 280 miles. As usual, Samuels was carrying on in a way to scare the wits out of his men, and as sometimes happens an extra big sea came rolling up. The dauntless "old man" had just time to shout a warning to the watch and to wedge himself under the bulwarks with one leg round a spare spar when the great comber washed aboard, high over everything.

It swept Samuels clean across the deck and left him hanging half over the leerail with a gashed head and a broken leg. He was knocked silly and would have gone overboard altogether if some of the crew had not reached him in time and pulled him in. And when he came to, this man of furious energy found himself lying a helpless cripple in a water-logged cabin, with the creaking and grinding of a rudder which was out of control sounding in his ears. It appears that the helmsmen had deserted the wheel in their fright and that the officers were more taken up with seeing to their captain than looking after the ship.

For a few moments there was pandemonium whilst the wheel spun back and forth as dangerous to handle as a whirling buzz-saw: then a tremendous jar was felt through the ship—the tiller had broken short off and the rudder had gone. Meanwhile Samuels, sweating with the pain of a compound fracture and in a fury at his own helplessness, actually determined to amputate the leg himself, there being no surgeon aboard; but luckily his officers had sufficient sense to dissuade him from this desperate resolve. Between them, they managed by dint of hard pulling to drag the crook out of the leg, though even so they could not get it quite straight. However, they made shift to lash it up sufficiently well to allow of Samuels being carried on deck to superintend the making of a jury rudder. Then for three days the *Dreadnought* lay in the trough of the sea whilst this makeshift was being fashioned.

At last it was ready. But now came the last straw. As it was being lowered overboard, the purchase carried away and down it went to the bottom of the sea. What followed is best told in Captain Samuels' own words:

"The ship was swinging with head to northward; it was calm weather, with the swell from the west. Fayal bore south by east magnetic, and during the afternoon a slight breeze sprang up from the west-south-west, westerly, and we did all we possibly could to turn the ship's head southward by using a drag from the starboard quarter, and by throwing another drag, consisting of a water-cask with one head out, from the starboard cat-head, as soon as the ship paid off. Each drag had a tendency to turn her to the eastward, we expecting finally to turn her to the southward, and thus to get her on the course to Fayal. It blew a royal breeze, and she paid off with her head sails, no sails being set aft, until she brought the wind well on her quarter; but after ten hours of strenuous effort we found it impossible to get her head in the proposed direction. So we took in the drags, furled all the head sails and all the canvas on the foremast, set all the square sails on the mizen mast, the whole of the main topsail and the starboard clew of the mainsail, and threw sharp aback every sail that was set. The tendency was to give her a stern board, *i.e.*, to sail her stern first. By keeping the sails trimmed flat aback on those two masts, the ship was backed 280 miles, the weather continuing mild and spring-like, the wind steady at west, and the ship's stern heading directly for Fayal, which then bore south magnetic. At this time we were able to ship our second rudder, and in a short time we entered Fayal harbour fourteen days after the disaster."

Here Samuels, lashed down on a mattress in a specially made box, was hoisted overboard by a tackle at the yardarm and lowered down into a boat alongside. As there was a sea running, the operation had to be conducted with care, the captain himself having to cut the slings that held him and this just at the right moment. This he managed to do without giving himself a heavy drop into the dancing boat. The next business was to get him ashore. It was too rough to land at the pier, and they finally had to row three miles down the beach and make a landing through the surf, after which the tortured man was carried up to the hotel.

The Portuguese surgeons wanted to operate at once, but Samuels would not allow it, insisting that he had not endured the last two weeks of agony in order to lose his leg, also that if he had meant to have it amputated he would have done it himself at the beginning. So they set the leg in splints, but so indifferently that the fractured bones were not brought together, and only the man's iron constitution pulled him through.

For 52 days he had to wait whilst his ship was undergoing her repairs. He might have gone home in another vessel, but all he owned in the world was in the *Dreadnought* and he would not leave her.

At last she was ready for sea. Samuels was slung aboard in his box; and a course set for Sandy Hook. On his arrival, Samuels found himself chained to a bed for eleven months; however, he had the consolation of knowing that he had saved his ship and saved his leg.

The Last Days of the "Dreadnought."

Owing to his broken leg Captain Samuels was reluctantly obliged to give up the command of the *Dreadnought* to Captain Lytle in 1863.

In December, 1863, on his return trip from Liverpool Captain Lytle was knocked down by a heavy sea and so badly injured that he died: the mate, Mr. Rockwell, took the ship into Fayal and then on to New York, where he arrived on 26th February, 1864. This was the "Flying Dutchman's" last Atlantic passage. The day of the Western Ocean packet was all but over, and the *Dreadnought* was put into the Cape Horn fleet.

Mr. Bradlee, in his pamphlet on the *Dreadnought*, gives the details of her last voyages.

In October, 1864, she arrived at San Francisco, 134 days out from New York, with Captain Cushing in command. From San Francisco she crossed to Honolulu in order to load whale oil. It was the custom for the South Sea whalers to unload their whale oil at Honolulu and then continue cruising in search of more. There was thus a demand for fast ships to bring this Honolulu-deposited oil home, and one of the first of the clippers to load whale oil at Honolulu was the famous *Sovereign of the Seas* on her maiden voyage.

The *Dreadnought*, with a full hold of oil barrels, made the fine run to New Bedford of 84 days, her best 24 hours work being 272 miles.

On her second Cape Horn voyage, still under Captain Cushing, she arrived in San Francisco Bay in January, 1866, 127 days out; from there she went to Callao in 44 days, and loaded home from the West Coast.

In July, 1868, she once again arrived at San Francisco with a Captain Callaghan in command, being 149 days out from New York.

Leaving San Francisco on 11th October, 1868, with grain for U.K., she called at Queenstown 121 days out and reached Liverpool, 125 days out.

The "Dreadnought" drifts on to the Rocks of Tierra del Fuego in a Calm.

In 1869 the *Dreadnought* again left New York for San Francisco under Captain Mayhew, and when approaching the Horn left her bones on the inhospitable shores of Tierra del Fuego. The famous old ship actually drifted ashore in a calm—surely a curious end for the "Wild Boat of the Atlantic."

The *Dreadnought* was making for the Straits of Le Maire, when a calm came on near the entrance to the Straits of Magellan. The sheer bleak coast of Tierra del Fuego was close aboard to starboard, with its frowning black gorges, steep snowclad crags and forbidding rocks. Inland a rolling veldt-like country could be seen, forming one of the finest sheep pasturages in the world, and beyond that rose a magnificent range of mountains dazzling white in their everlasting snows.

There was a heavy swell running, which could be seen and heard as it foamed and thundered on the rock-bound coast. The *Dreadnought* had all sail set to her main skysail, but there was not a breath of wind, and the sails threatened to flog themselves to tatters as they clattered into the masts at every roll.

A strong current sets through the Straits of Le Maire and along the coast—this it was suddenly noticed was carrying the ship inshore. There was no possibility of anchoring, the coast being steep to with only a few places where ships could be brought up. There was nothing to do but hope that the wind would come along quickly. But there was no sign of wind; one of those Cape Horn breathing spells of calm gripped the *Dreadnought* in its mournful, eerie embrace.

And her drift inshore seemed to grow more and more

rapid. At last, when the matter was almost desperate, the covers were torn off the boats on the skids and they were feverishly slung overboard, whilst all hands piled into them in a hopeless attempt to tow the ship clear. To tow a heavy 1400-ton ship, fully loaded, in a Cape Horn swell is a sheer impossibility, but one can picture the sight and feel the furious panic of those men as they tugged at the long oars and were jerked back at every stroke as the tow lines tautened and slacked with every long roller which ran under the boats.

At last the crash came, and the famous ship brought up on the black fangs of Tierra del Fuego, having sailed her last traverse.

The next three weeks were spent by her crew with all the usual sufferings of shipwrecked men, exposed to the inclement elements of that latitude. Added to which they had ever to be on watch against possible attacks from the wild Tierra del Fuegians, the most primitive savages in the whole world. In order to guard against a surprise the *Dreadnoughts* put to sea in their boats every night and only landed at daylight in order to get a little sleep and cook what food they had, also in order to keep a lookout for ships.

At last at the end of three weeks they were picked up by a passing ship, and the *Dreadnought* was left to go slowly to pieces in the grip of the surf.

So much for the "Wild Boat of the Atlantic," a sailing ship which has been more talked about and sung about than perhaps any other in the history of man.

Then a health to the *Dreadnought*, and to her brave crew,
To bold Captain Samuels and his officers too.
Talk about your flash packets, Swallow Tail and Black Ball,
The *Dreadnought's* the flier that can lick them all.

Cope's Philadelphia Line.

There is just one more line of packet ships which deserves mention, and that is the Philadelphia Line started by Thomas P. Cope as far back as 1807, the ships being mostly built by John Lynn of Philadelphia and his descendants.

The first ship of this line was the little *Lancaster* of 290 tons built in 1807; she was followed by the *Tuscarora* of 349 tons in 1810.

By the forties the Philadelphia Line had some big ships on the Atlantic, and the rate asked for a cabin passage was £20.

A good many of Cope's ships loaded cotton from New Orleans, a very big sailing ship trade in the old days with a history of its own, though there was very little difference, if any, between the New Orleans cotton ships and the rest of the Atlantic packets.

Some of the best known of the Philadelphia packets were the following:—*Saranac*, 854 tons, built 1844; *Wyoming*, 912 tons; *Tonawanda*, 1503 tons; *Monongahela*; 509 tons; *Susquehanna*, 600 tons; *Thomas B. Cope*, 800 tons, all built in the forties. *Tuscarora* II. 1449 tons, built 1848; *John H. Jervis*, 1790 tons; and *Chimera*, 1300, both built in 1852, the last two being for the New Orleans trade. Cope provided a monthly service and his line lasted for about half a century.

The Largest of the Packet Ships.

According to Bradlee, a second *Ocean Monarch* launched at New York in 1856 was the largest packet built. She measured 2145 tons and was 240 feet long. No other packet came near her in size.

The *Charles H. Marshall*, 1600 tons, built in 1869 by Wm. H. Webb, was the last packet built for the Black Ball Line.

The last ships of the Black X Line were the *Palestine* and *Amazon*, of 1800 tons, built in 1854.

The *Palestine*, under Captain J. M. Lord, once landed her passengers at Plymouth in 14 days, having beaten the Cunarder in the run across.

I think the biggest ship built for the Swallow Tail was the *New World*, of 1404 tons: she was also one of the last of the packets to remain in the service.

The *Ne Plus Ultra*, of 1300 tons, Captain Borden, was actually the last packet ship running. She belonged to the Black X Line, and her last trans-Atlantic passage was in 1883.

The big *City of Mobile*, built by Perrine and Stack at Greenpoint in 1854 for Harbeck & Co., of New York, was more of a carrier than a passenger packet. She measured 1750 tons with a length of 215 feet, and her portrait shows her with the early double topsails, when the foot of the upper topsail was often laced to the lower topsail yard. She had three decks and was a big grain carrier, taking 9000 quarters of wheat to England on her maiden trip. However, she is classed amongst the American packets and no doubt carried emigrants.

"CITY OF MOBILE."

"MASSACHUSETTS."

In a squall, November 10, 1845.

From the MacPherson Collection.

PART II.

'E's a man that's shipped for fightin', 'cos 'is fists is iron bound,
'An, generally speakin', you'd find 'is wind is sound.
'E's a dandy with a slung shot, an' you'd 'ave to travel far
Before you'd find 'is equal with a 'eavy capstan-bar.

'Is voice is like an angry bull's—'e 'ardly ever smiles,
An' when 'e yells an order it'll carry fifteen miles.
'E mostly sails in packet ships, where hours are long an' 'ard,
'An 'alf the crowd are carried in a fightin' after-guard.
                    (*From "The Bucko Mate" by J. St. A. Jewell*).

The Life of a Packet Ship.

IT was extraordinary the way the wooden packet ships stood the cracking on: the Yankee clippers were many of them strained all to pieces in a few years, yet the packets stayed with it, year after year, punching valiantly back and forth across the Western Ocean.

Here is the record of a famous Black Baller, taken from the *New York Herald*. She was on the Atlantic for 29 years, and made 116 round voyages "without losing a seaman, a sail or a spar." "She had brought 30,000 passengers" to America, and had been the scene of "1500 births and 200 marriages."

And after such a life she quietly went on for many more years in the American coasting trade.

A Method of Stopping Leaks.

There was one trouble which had to be contended with in driving these wooden packets. They were liable to strain the caulking out of the seams. There was an old sailors' remedy for this, which was to cut up a barrel or so of rope-yarns and throw them overboard around the ship. Suction was supposed to carry the yarns into the seams and so stop the leaks.

This remedy was once tried by Captain Urquhart. He hove his ship to, cast the rope-yarns overboard, and for a time the experiment acted; but he declared that the yarns worked out again in two or three days and the ship leaked as badly as ever.

He also tells this story of a leaking packet. The vessel in question, when about 600 miles from New York, on her way to Liverpool, became so leaky as to be in a sinking condition. All hands were working desperately at the pumps, when the captain spoke up: "If the water continues to gain upon the pumps as it does now we shall all be in eternity before morning. I am going below to pray, and ask if anyone wishes to join me."

The men replied, "You pray, captain, and we'll pump." An hour later and the pumps began to gain on the leak, and in the end were sucked dry. After this it only required a little extra pumping to keep the ship free of water.

The captain was as surprised as his crew at this sudden change, but he always declared that his praying stopped the leak. The ship was docked on her arrival, and it was then found that a strip of seaweed, 2 feet long, was stuck fast in a seam and had thus stopped the leak and saved the ship.

How to Avoid being Pooped.

Another device of these experienced captains was occasionally resorted to, when running before a dangerously big sea in heavy weather, in order to avoid being pooped by a breaking hill of water.

A stout manila cable was paid out from one quarter and taken in at the other. The bight of the cable was thus dragged beneath the surface at a depth that could be easily regulated by the amount paid out in relation to the speed of the vessel, but about 6 feet below the surface was considered to be the most satisfactory. The chasing seas when they reached the submerged cable were broken by it and, toppling over, ran on in a mass of foam which swirled round the packet's stern and frothed by on each quarter, but without weight and therefore without danger to the ship.

It is said that this device, though it must have somewhat reduced a ship's speed, was very successful in preventing any heavy water being pooped. At the same time it gave the helmsman confidence and ease of mind, for there is probably no more nerve-racking ordeal than that of steering a heavy, hard-mouthed ship before a big, nasty sea. The very best helmsman knows that, however skilful he may be, he may not be able to prevent that monster of a greybeard, the ninth or the tidal wave, from breaking over the poop with a force which may mean death to himself, a broken wheel and a broach to.

The Captains of the Yankee Packets—Men of Steel.

There were no finer seamen afloat than the captains and officers of the Yankee packets; yet there has always been one black spot on their otherwise splendid records: they were "hard citizens." They had to be in such a life and with such crews, but there is no doubt that many of them, nay, the majority of them, carried their hardness too far. Their discipline was a false discipline. They ruled by sheer physical force, without the least glimmer of that spark of sympathy without which men cannot be led but only driven. And drive their men they surely did, with that fierce mercilessness with which they drove their ships—and with a nerve which only a sea-training can produce.

Yet from the first these hard Yankee captains were drawn from a higher and more educated class than the general run of mercantile officers in other nations, with the exception, of course, of East Indiamen.

Here is a quotation from Lindsey, being the report of Consul Peter of Philadelphia:

"A lad intending for the higher grades of the Merchant Service in this country, after having been at school for some years and acquired (in addition to the ordinary branches of school learning) a competent knowledge of mathematics, navigation, ship's-husbandry and perhaps French, is generally apprenticed to some respectable merchant, in whose counting house he remains two or three years, or at least until he becomes

familiar with exchanges and such other commercial
matters as may best qualify him to represent his
principal in foreign countries. He is then sent to sea,
generally in the capacity of second mate, from which
he gradually rises to that of captain."

The captains of the packets nearly always had a
share in their ships, and instead of a regular salary
lived on their primage. In the best days this often
came to 5000 dollars a year, and was made up as follows:
—5 per cent. on all freight money, 25 per cent. on all
cabin passage money, 5 per cent. on all steerage passage
money, and the whole of the mail allowance, which was
twopence a letter from the British Government and two
cents a letter from the American. In addition to this
the captain condescended to take a small fixed salary
of 360 dollars a year, if he did not happen to possess
shares in his ship.

On board ship his power was absolute, whilst ashore
he met the owners and shipping merchants on terms of
equality, and his family moved in the same circle of
society as those of his owners.

It may be concluded from Consul Peter's report that
these American captains learnt half their trade ashore
before going to sea; yet if this mercantile training
explains their shrewdness and capability for ships'
business, it does not show reason for their fine seamanship any more than the fine manners of the lordly
captain ashore coincide with his, I fear, often desperately brutal demeanour at sea.

Skipper's Boast of their "Man-eating"
Mates.

It has been stated that Yankee captains rarely interfered with the working of their ships and never condescended to man-handle their crews themselves.

This aloofness may have been considered the correct thing but, as we shall see later on, it was far from being a hard and fast rule. And if most of them did refrain from taking a hand personally in the taming of their crews they yet gave every encouragement to their bucko officers and took a queer pride in the possession of a reputation for cruel usage. Indeed, it is a curious fact that the captain of a noted "slaughter-house" or "blood-boat" was often the centre of admiration and envy ashore. And he would boast of his exploits with that graphic power of illustration which is such a feature of the American tongue.

The following instance will give some idea of this Yankee delight in a tough reputation:—

Scene, room in a shipping office along the East River, New York. A hard-faced, fire-eating packet captain is holding forth to an admiring crowd of the shipping fraternity and describing his last voyage. After giving a lurid account of some of his disciplinary measures he casually ends up with the statement that it was his practice to spread the toughest packet-rat on a ship's biscuit and eat him whenever he close-reefed his topsails, that his mate was a cross between a New Orleans mule and a wild cat, the greaser a reg'lar hellion from the word "go," and his third blower and striker a full-grown man-eating tiger who blooded his whiskers every change of the watch.

Probably amongst his audience there would be another fire-eater who was also a bit of a humorist. This one would then begin with true American guile.

"Your packet's sure enough hot stuff, mate. Compared with your crate o' wild cats my officers don't cut no ice: still, they ain't so slow, and I reckon my third blower and striker ain't no Nancy in kid gloves—"

"Who is he?" grunts some one in the office.

"Waal," with that slow drawl which drives a point home with such effect, "I'm a humane man, as you know, and he's a bit too hot-handed for me; I callate I'll have to get rid of him."

"How's that?" from an eager listener, whilst the first captain scowls round with an air of infinite boredom.

"Waal, it's this way," goes on number two serenely, "he came near bankrupting me in oil last passage."

"What?"

"Yes, that's so. You see where he touched a man it always left a burn. And some o' my raynecks swore they were scorched six foot away. His name, you say? His name was Jonathan D. Satan !!"

"Knocking Down" and "Dragging Out" aboard the "Devonshire."

That this excessive hazing of their crews did not pay the better class of packet officer understood only too well, yet, until the end, it was persisted in by the majority, especially on those ships whose commanders had risen from the foc's'le, and such officers were by no means as uncommon as Consul Peter's report would lead one to suppose.

The following instance, which I have taken from a little book of reminiscences written by a packet captain, goes to prove that where a ship was notorious for ill treatment her master was the person responsible for it.

"In the ship *Devonshire*, a Black X London liner, I was chief officer in 1859. The captain knew that I was opposed to this abominable abuse (of the men) so he found a second officer of his own kind, who was a regular bull-terrier. He got the men so scared of him they were completely bewildered in working the ship, pulled the wrong ropes and upset things generally. I pointed out to him the error of this foolish sort of hazing and told him I had tried his plan and knew from experience there was a better way to handle men, and he said he believed as I did. But at the time he shipped the captain had told him what would suit him, and in his watch on deck when I was below the captain encouraged him in 'knocking down and dragging out,' as that sort of treatment was commonly called.

"One dark night in a gale a sailor fell from the main topsail yard while reefing, and was lost. The crew all left on arrival in London, and reported that the second officer had kicked this man overboard. He was arrested and partially tried in London, when it was decided that English courts had no jurisdiction over a murder on the high seas under the American flag. He was then sent to New York a prisoner, tried and convicted of

"DEVONSHIRE."

New York and London Packet Ship.

From a Lithograph in possession of the Author.

"DREADNOUGHT."

Off Sandy Hook, February 23, 1854—19 days from Liverpool.

From a Lithograph in possession of the Author.

man-slaughter in a degree that gave him three years' imprisonment.

"The captain was denounced severely in the London court for his cruelty and came near being placed under arrest himself."

"Bucko" Mates versus "Packet-Rats."

I do not wish to leave the impression that there was nothing to be said in extenuation of this rough treatment of the men. There is, indeed, a great deal to be said from the officers' side of the deck. The captain had to make good passages and the officers had to carry out heavy work in the worst weather with material which was composed of the dregs of the world's seafaring population, with a sprinkling of criminals and landsmen thrown in. And as every sailorman knows, sail carrying means man driving unless the foremast complement is both efficient in knowledge and sufficient in numbers. This was far from being the case in the later packet ships.

And when one remembers that the bucko officers had been ground in the mill themselves and hardened in the hardest school in the world, can one wonder at the iron fist? Of course, the iron fist frequently went too far, as, for instance, when it was exchanged for iron belaying pin or that instrument of torture known as the "persuader," a stick about a yard long with a sharp nail projecting half an inch from its end. But I will give an instance or two of tough crews to show the necessity of shipping officers "who could whip their own weight in wild cats," as the saying was.

Captain Samuels and the Bloody Forty.

The first is the story of Captain Samuels and the Bloody Forty.

"In those days," wrote the old packet skipper, "we had a class of sailors who shipped by the run. As their pay was invariably drawn in advance, it was always a case of 'working out a dead horse,' as we used to say. The men were inclined to do little work, and they had to be driven. It took a rigid and often a severe man to master them.

"Chief amongst these 'packetarians' was the 'Bloody Forty,' a regularly organised set of men, with headquarters in Liverpool. Many crimes were charged to them, and the latest cruelty laid at their door just previous to their shipping with me was the brutal killing of Captain Bryer, of the Black Ball packet *Columbia*."

It was in July, 1859, that 30 out of the "Bloody Forty" signed on with Captain Samuels. Several of this gang of packet-rats had already sailed with the captain of the *Dreadnought* on previous occasions and had old scores to settle.

Packet-rats invariably came aboard a ship "flying light"—in other words with an empty kit bag—this bag was usually crammed to overflowing at the end of the passage, the old hands having either stolen or bullied clothes and bedding, oilskins and sea boots from the first voyagers or joskins. Samuels, being experienced in all the ways of packet-rats, made it a rule to have these well-filled bags emptied and the clothes restored to their rightful owners at the end of every passage. This was just one reason why the Bloody Forty decided to put things to the touch with the redoubtable skipper.

Captain Samuels gives another reason. He stated that the gang were tired of the Western Ocean and intended to capture a ship and turn pirates, or "go on the account" as their grandfathers would have called it; and that they chose the *Dreadnought* on account of her speed.

Mansfield, the Liverpool magistrate—who had often shipped boys with Captain Samuels instead of sending them to gaol, not, as one might suppose, after reading Doctor Johnson's dictum, as a punishment, but in order that they might be reformed by the stern ship-master—warned Captain Samuels that his detectives had got wind of a plot against the *Dreadnought's* captain, which had been hatched in the den of a notorious sailor's boarding-house keeper, named Mrs. Riley.

But Samuels remained serene and unmoved. He boasted that he had never yet rejected a crew on account of their bad character and frequently found them to be the best sailors.

So on 11th July, 1859, the *Dreadnought* left the Waterloo Dock with the Bloody Forty on board. When off the Rock Light Samuels anchored in order to take on board his steerage passengers and his only cabin passenger, a woman.

At the last moment the crew were mustered and

inspected by Captain Schomberg, the emigration agent; at the same instant a gig pulled hurriedly alongside, and a messenger from the magistrate jumped aboard the *Dreadnought* and besought the captain not to put to sea with this gang of cut-throats in his foc's'le.   Schomberg also recognised the leaders of the gang, Finnegan, Sweeney and Casey and urged Samuels to put them ashore.

The old man's reply came in his usual downright fashion:—

"I'll see them in Hades and pumping thunder before I'll sail without them.   Never fear, I'll draw their teeth."   He then turned to the men and roared:— "Here you men, line up here and step lively.   You have all got pointed knives.   Don't deny it!   The carpenter will break the points.   That's the rule of the ship.   Go to the carpenter's shop."   Only Sweeney dared to ask: "What for?"   "You, Sweeney," bellowed the captain, "another word, and I'll have you against the shrouds."

This was greeted by hisses, but apparently the men went forward and had the points broken off their knives.   But their grumblings were plainly audible aft, and the fierce old skipper immediately sang out in his reef-topsail voice: "Lay aft here, all hands."   Then whilst Samuels lectured the Bloody Forty in his own picturesque style, his officers searched the fo'c'sle for weapons.

According to Samuels both Finnegan and Casey had sailed with him before, whilst the skipper and Sweeney had been in Mobile gaol together, when Samuels was a boy.

As soon as the mates had finished their search the windlass was manned. The tug cast off at Point Lynas, and the *Dreadnought* was tacked across the Irish Sea against a moderate S.W. wind.

On the 12th July the wind backed to the southward and the *Dreadnought* was able to lay her course.

At noon, when off Queenstown, whilst the crew were at dinner, old Samuels noticed that the helmsman was constantly off his course. "Steer steady," came his order. The man at the wheel made no reply.

"I spoke to you, now reply," roared Samuels, showing temper.

At this the helmsman took his hands off the wheel, and facing the old man, replied sullenly:—"You're wrong. I am steering steady."

This was too much for the old man's rising irritation. He sprang at the helmsman, who grabbed his sheath knife, but was too late; out went the captain's fist and the man dropped senseless alongside the wheel. Then, whilst the skipper's dog, Wallace, a magnificent Newfoundland, stood guard over the fallen helmsman, with his paws on the man's chest, Samuels dashed down the companionway for the handcuffs, bellowing for Whitehorn, the second mate. When the captain and his second officer reached the deck, they found the struggling helmsman being held down by the dog; after a further brief struggle, the handcuffs were slipped on and the man locked up in the after house.

As his sheath knife was found to be pointed, Samuels concluded that "the crew intended to clip the ship's wings and make me swim." He thereupon called his officers, together with the carpenter and cook, into the cabin. Parker, his first officer, had lately been in command of a packet but was sailing with Samuels for the first time.

"Men, it's a case of the foc's'le agin the cabin. There are 40 to 6 of us. How do you stand?" asked the captain. But let me give the incident in his own words.

" 'Seeing as I'm the senior officer I'll speak first, and brief,' began Parker excitedly; "I'll do no fighting.'

" 'Then, you dirty cur, you're no officer of mine,' I shouted, almost tempted to keep him from the mess.

" 'Aye, so be it,' he replied meekly, as he started to leave. But I stopped him.

" 'One minute there, you Parker; I want you to see what a coward you are. Back up into that corner and maybe you'll learn something.' Whitehorn was the next. Although a small man, his face showed the stuff he was made of. He took a step forward, saluted, and then, extending his hand, said quietly, "You know me, captain.' The third mate, a middle-aged man, named Hooker, was the next. 'Well?' I enquired impatiently.

" 'I'm afraid I'm a little old, and—'

" 'Never mind,' I broke in, fully aroused. 'You and Parker can report to the galley. Git!' 'Now, you two shellbacks' (I addressed the carpenter and cook), ' what can I expect ? '

"The cook, a big fat fellow, slapped his hands on his stomach as much as to say—'this would be in the way.' The carpenter said that he did not sign on to fight, and fight he would not. I got rid of them, ordering them not to show their faces above deck.

"When they had gone, Whitehorn turned to me. 'Captain, I'm willing,' he said, 'but I haven't a weapon except an old pepperbox pistol.'

"'Fill her up, pull the trigger and trust to God,' I replied."

By this time, with Samuels holding a council of war aft, and Finnegan and Sweeney preparing their forces for battle forward, the unhappy emigrants, as usual with non-combatants, were in a pretty state of panic. According to the skipper, "the Norwegians were praying one kind of prayer, the Germans another, and the Hungarians were singing theirs." Then the steward reported that the only cabin passenger, the wife of a prominent New York attorney, was missing. After a two hours search she was found under a couch.

As soon as the cabin conference was over, Captain Samuels gave the order:—"Haul taut the weather main brace !" The men trooped aft, but instead of tailing on to the brace scowled fiercely up at the old man.

"Why don't you obey the order, you blundering murderers?" roared the irate skipper.

"Let Mike out of irons first," spoke Finnegan, the

leader of the Bloody Forty, whom Samuels described as "one of the toughest men I ever met."

"Not if I had a thousand of you in irons," yelled the old man, shaking his fist at the crew.

"Then you'll holystone hell," retorted Finnegan amidst a torrent of curses.

In one account the captain wrote that the crowd now pulled out their knives and advanced upon him, but in a second account he makes no mention of this, and states that as he turned to go below in order to arm himself the crew ran forward. As the second account seems to have been generally toned down from the first I will follow that.

Apparently the helmsman had left the wheel to join the men, and the second mate had taken the wheel. The other two officers were probably below, whilst the emigrants were apprehensively watching the fracas from abreast the mainmast—they were not allowed on the quarterdeck—and before jumping below for his guns Captain Samuels ordered them to go below.

As Samuels appeared at the break of the poop, with a levelled revolver in each hand, the men were just starting up the ladders.

"Move an inch, one of you," hissed the captain, "and we'll have the burial service in short order."

"The devil you will," sneered Finnegan, flourishing his knife. "You're too much of a coward, you damned psalm-singing—"

"Move back there!" interrupted old Samuels. Not a man stirred.

"Shoot!" jeered Finnegan defiantly, ripping off his shirt and bearing his breast. "Shoot now, you dirty, low-livered coward!"

The captain levelled his weapon upon the leader of the Bloody Forty, but the man never moved an eyelid.

This roused the old man to fury. "I could kill you, Finnegan, you cur," he began, then went on with rising voice; "but I'm going to starve everyone of you into submission instead. Do you hear? I'll make you get down on your knees and beg for mercy."

Howls and jeers greeted this outburst, and Casey broke in:—"Kill the old fool now." But the weaker members of the foc's'le had had enough of this bluff, and began to sneak away. Finally Finnegan, Sweeney, and Casey were left standing alone.

Then, with many a curse, they swung on their heels and retired to the foc's'le. All that night Samuels paced the quarterdeck with his faithful dog by his side, whilst the second mate and boys attended to any sail trimming that was needed. At daybreak a report spread through the ship that the crew had barricaded themselves in the foc's'le.

At noon, the order "Take in the royals" was roared from aft. But beyond a muffled "Go to hell" from the interior of the foc's'le no notice was taken. As the wind was freshening fast, the sails were furled by the officers and boys. The ship was then headed off to the N.N.W.

By midnight it was blowing hard with a nasty sea making, into which the *Dreadnought* was pitching foc's'le under whilst a roaring flood frothed in the lee scuppers. The ship was going a good 12 knots, and never had she had such a dusting. The topgallant sails were lowered to the caps, but Samuels dared not touch his topsails for want of man power. Luckily the wind began to moderate at 4 a.m. and by 8 bells it was nearly calm. As soon as the topgallant sails were set, Samuels went forward in an attempt to turn the crew to.

The reply to his demand was a request for something to eat before turning to. But the old man was of a different mind. "You shall work before you eat," he yelled through the bulkhead. At this there were howls of execration, and sounds as of the barricade being removed, whereupon the fierce old man thought it wise to beat a retreat.

At 7 bells that morning a committee of the passengers came aft and demanded that the crew should be fed. According to Samuels, they were under the delusion that he was maltreating his crew.

Every hair on the old man bristled up at this interference, and he started in to read the committee a lecture on the subject of mutiny. But he was interrupted by one of his listeners, who, greatly daring, broke in with:—"If you won't feed the crew, we will."

"If you do I'll put you in irons," yelled the skipper.

"You can't do it," retorted the other hotly. Roaring to the second mate to go for the handcuffs, Samuels grappled with his defiant passenger. The latter struck out and missed. In a moment the captain had him by the throat, and after a sharp scuffle the handcuffs were again called into duty.

This was the end of any interference by the passengers. At sunset the sea was smooth, the wind a nice breeze from the N.W., and the ship logging 8 knots close-hauled. Once more the old man went forward to parley with the crew, and offered to forget their mutinous conduct if they would throw their knives overboard and go to work, but he was careful to except Finnegan. Sweeney and Casey from this amnesty.

Once more his offer was received with yells of defiance.

The crew had now been fifty-six hours without food, and Samuels realised that the crisis was not far off. So, at 8 bells, 8 p.m., he left the second mate in charge of the deck, with orders to shoot the first man who came abaft the mainmast, whilst he descended to the after steerage in order to enlist the help of the German emigrants.

Addressing them in their own language, he was soon able to recruit 17 sturdy Dutchies, whom he armed with iron bars taken from the cargo. These he ordered to remain below, ready to jump on deck at the first call.

Towards midnight whilst the captain and Whitehorn were pacing the quarterdeck, with Wallace, the dog, in their wake, the dog began to growl; two men were then discovered crawling aft, and the captain thought he caught the gleam of knife blades in their hands.

"Shall I shoot?" asked the second mate anxiously.

"No," hissed the captain.

"Shall I slip down and call up the Germans?"

"No, wait," ordered the old man. They waited until the two men were abreast of the capstan, which was about 20 feet away, and then the old man's cyclonic voice broke the peace of the calm night.

"Halt! Stand up and let me see who you are or I'll put a bullet through you." Then, to the mate:— "Keep a watch down the gangway, these fellows are up to some trick."

"No, we're not, captain," replied one of the men, "we're ready to surrender if you'll take us back.

"Throw your knives overboard then," came the command. The men did so, and after the second mate had searched them and found nothing, Samuels proceeded to cross-examine them.

Ever since the crew had retired to the foc's'le they had kept a watch on the proceedings aft, four men going on duty at a time. These two men formed half of the foc's'le watch that was then on duty. According to them the other pair were also ready to give in. They told Samuels that everyone forward had taken an oath to kill him if he dared to come forward of the midshiphouse during the night, and that it was planned to burst in the galley at 8 bells so as to get food. Further, that one of the men had been knocked senseless with a serving mallet by Sweeney for suggesting surrender.

Captain Samuels now made final preparations for victory. The Germans were brought up and stationed round the deckhouse. The port ladder on to the poop was barricaded with the pigsty, whilst the steerage ladders were hauled up and the hatches closed, thus making prisoners of the emigrants below.

With all his preparations completed, the old man, backed by his second officer and his invaluable dog, started forward to investigate. It was a little after 7 bells in the middle watch, and at 8 bells the four men who had offered to surrender were to be relieved by Casey, Sweeney and two others, who meant to attack the galley and storeroom.

When abreast of the midshiphouse, the dog warned his master by a deep growl. Then out sprang Casey and Sweeney with lifted knives. Apparently both Samuels and his second mate thought discretion the better part of valour. In the words of the old man: "I ran back for some distance, until I got Casey where I wanted him —in front of my revolver. Whitehorn ran back to prepare the Germans."

But the dog sprang straight at Sweeney and knocked him over. Sweeney was up again in an instant, yelling:—"Come on, boys, we've got him."

With wild shouts the Bloody Forty hurled themselves to the attack, and in a moment the ship was in a pandemonium.

The emigrants, battened down below, and terrified at the noise on deck, shrieked and howled in a manner to rouse the dead.

On the port side of the house an outburst of cursing and the sound of blows told of the Germans who were holding back Finnegan and some half-dozen men. Others came clambering over the top of the house. But the iron bars of the Germans and the captain's pistols soon brought the struggle to a halt.

As the Bloody Forty drew back, Samuels roared out:— "I'll give you one minute to throw your knives overboard."

Finnegan, who had escaped the iron bolts of the Germans, now wormed his way to the front, and, defiant as ever, sang out:—"You shall be the first to go, you d——d psalm-singing old humbug."

"I'll settle with you later, Finnegan," returned the captain.

Then a man stepped forward and asked:—"If we throw our knives overboard what guarantee have we that you won't shoot us."

"I'll make no bargain until you throw away your knives."

"Here goes my knife," cried a man, standing just behind Finnegan, upon which the latter turned quickly and struck him full in the face. But Finnegan's authority was fast waning, and one by one the knives went spinning overboard. And when Sweeney and Casey had parted with theirs, only Finnegan's remained —at last with bad grace Finnegan also threw a knife over the side.

"Now," said the very much relieved skipper sternly, "I've got a score to settle with you, Finnegan, you're the first man to call me a coward, and now you've got to take it back."

"Not on your life," returned the undaunted Finnegan. But he was rash. Before the words were out of his

"IVANHOE."

1300 tons; built by Webb, 1849.

From the MacPherson Collection.

"NEW WORLD."

From a Drawing by Captain Paton.

mouth, the old man struck at him and knocked him, head foremost, down the foc's'le ladder. At this the men flared up again. Sweeney stooped down to draw a knife from the top of his boot.

But Samuels was too quick for him. "Up with your hands, all of you," he roared, and then commanded the second mate to search them again. Knives were found on Sweeney and Casey. Then Finnegan was hauled senseless out of the foc's'le, and a knife was found on him.

Captain Samuels now turned upon the thoroughly cowed Bloody Forty, and repeated his old order, which for two days and more had never been carried out, "Haul taut the weather main brace." The men tailed on, according to Samuels, as if they would spring the yard.

The day was breaking and the mutiny over, Samuels sent an order to the cook to get the men's coffee ready, and told the mate to set them to holystoning the decks as soon as they had had it.

Meanwhile Finnegan was brought round by the ship's doctor. As soon as he could sit up, the old man once more ordered him to apologise.

But Finnegan remained silent—it is possible that he was too dazed to speak.

I will now quote from Captain Samuels' book:— "I ordered him backed and put into the sweat box. In less than half an hour he cried for mercy, and was ready to say and do anything to be let out of irons."

The unrelenting old man had him led up to where all hands were holystoning the deck.

"Now, men, listen to what your leader and bully has to say," spoke Samuels.

"Captain," said Finnegan, "I have had enough. To say this does not make a coward of a man when he has found his master."

"That won't do," objected Samuels. "You must take back your insulting language."

"Well, then, captain, any man who says you're a coward is a liar."

This apparently satisfied the relentless old man. The handcuffs were taken off and Finnegan set to holystoning with the rest.

They were kept at this pleasant task the whole day— as the captain said—to make up for lost time. For the rest of the passage these suddenly reformed villains were as meek as so many lambs, and appeased their captain most effectually by attending Divine Service on the Sunday.

Later Samuels took the opportunity of lecturing the Bloody Forty on the evil ways of their life in true mid-Victorian style. "I ended with a prayer," he wrote in his book afterwards; "which brought tears to the eyes of most of these hardened men."

Human nature is a mass of contradictions and life is very like the weather, storm and calm with a few steady breezes; in weathering it out, one has only to lose one's balance through the lack of a small peg of ballast to fall from one extreme to another.

Before the passage was over that hard nut of an old man behaved more like a Methodist preacher than the captain of a notorious Yankee packet, whilst the Bloody Forty were not only eating out of his hand but even Finnegan was attempting to play the cast of the reformed bad man.

When the *Dreadnought* arrived off quarantine, wild stories of the mutiny spread through the city, and Superintendent Kennedy and a posse of police hurried down to the docks just in time to see the bloodthirsty mutineers bidding goodbye to their captain, with three hearty cheers.

Captain Trask of the "Saratoga."

Captain Trask of the *Saratoga* was another of those iron-nerved skippers who could deal with a tough crew. On one occasion he left Havre with a foc's'le full of French convicts, just out of gaol. His mate fell ill and died. The men gradually grew more and more insubordinate. Then the moment came and Trask acted. A man was openly mutinous. Trask immediately put him in irons. At this the rest came aft, bent on making trouble. Trask's second mate was his own son. He ordered him to run a line across the deck, and on the crew showing signs of rushing this line, instead of obeying his order to go forward, he faced them with a revolver, calling out: "The first man who passes that rope I'll shoot. I am going to call you one by one, and if two come forward together I will shoot both." With this strong hint to be careful, he immediately called out a man. The fellow hesitated.

"I'll give you one more chance," said Trask calmly.

It was enough. His grit told. The man caved in, and was put in irons as soon as he had crossed the rope. In this way, one by one, Trask put the irons on 18 men. He then made them lie flat on their stomachs on the floor of the cabin. Upon which the chains of their handcuffs were stapled to the deck. And the last scene of this high seas drama is perhaps the most significant of all. It shows Trask fast asleep on the cabin settee, wholly indifferent to the scowling faces and wriggling forms of the eighteen mutineers in irons on the floor.

Towing to Sea.

It was at the start of a passage that most of the trouble between officers and crew took place. The crew were invariably dazed with drink, and very often the officers were turned into fiends by sundry nips from the poison which they found in the foc's'le. For, as soon as the ship was under weigh, it was customary to muster the hands aft for a call over, watch-picking and the usual piece of oratory by the captain; and, whilst this was progressing, one of the afterguard rummaged the foc's'le for liquor, guns, knives, etc. Then as soon as the captain had made his little speech, which was always short and to the point, the mates had to make sail. Now came the fun of the fair: and in a notorious "blood-boat" it was slaughter from the word "go," whilst even in the more humanely-run packet a fight was almost a certainty, especially when leaving the American side.

Here is a "towing to sea" from the mate's side of the deck.

"Once, going down the river from the Shadwell Basin, London Docks, one tug alongside and another ahead, the second mate had some words with one of his men, who plunged his knife into the second mate's stomach. In a few seconds we were fighting the whole crew. I was standing near the carpenter (who was caulking the main hatch prior to putting a deckhouse over it) when one of the men came behind me with a capstan bar, which he raised on high to strike me on the head; however, the carpenter was the quicker and brought his caulking mallet down on the small of the man's back, doubling him up. The chief steward with a revolver in one hand and an iron belaying pin in the other settled one or two more, and soon we had them running round the deck away from us: nearly all of them got over the side into the tug, and then into her stokehold: one man jumped overboard to swim ashore and was drowned. At Gravesend the second mate and two men were sent ashore to the Infirmary, where he and one sailor died."

The brother of the narrator of this experience, when mate of the *New World*, was once compelled to shoot a man dead in self-defence. In such affairs it was a case of "I'm your meat or you're mine," and only a ready use of the "six-gun" saved the numerically inferior party from extermination.

The officers of the packet ships were paid from 30 to 60 dollars a month according to their rank, and there is no doubt that they earned it—every cent of it.

The Psychology of the Bucko Mate.

The psychology of the bucko mate is a very interesting study, being much akin to that of the old time Wild West desperado.

I have met and known both species and found them much like anyone else under the hard crust which they presented to the world, though great force of character was undoubtedly the mainspring of their strange natures.   They were the survivors of the fittest in a life which gave no quarter to the weakling, and a certain inborn grit accounted for their position of leadership over their fellows.   Yet with great self-control and coolness in moments of great danger, the bucko deliberately abandoned all self-control in his methods of discipline, and drove his watch in a white heat of Berserker temper and vicious spite—the last very often the result of nerves irritated and tried beyond all bearing.

There were various factors which encouraged the bucko in his methods.   One of these was a queer pride in proving himself a tough citizen—a man-handler— an ogre who knew no mercy.   Another was more laudable—the necessity of the ship and the dominating thought which put her first in everything and made unceasing toil as well as hard knocks and bitter recriminations all part of the scheme—a necessary of packet ship life and one which could not be avoided if a mate's duty was to be properly carried out.

But when all has been said, the fact remains that the bucko was the direct result of the extraordinarily hard

conditions of the life.   He usually had to fight his way
up, from the foc's'le to the quarterdeck through the
various grades of ship's boy, rayneck, packet-rat and
bosun.   These man-drivers are often full of complex
contradictions.   In the performance of their duties
cruel as an Iroquois and hard as so much flint, in private
life they were often as simple as children and as easily
moved to laughter or tears, with a soft streak which
would show up when least expected.   Sometimes a
wonderful tenderness and love for animals went hand in
hand with a callous indifference regarding human beings.

One of the best hearted men I ever knew was the
renowned bucko mate of a notorious "blood-boat" for
some years.   I asked him why he left it to sail under the
more easy-going red duster: he answered that he sickened
at the blood, the blood which was spilt every watch
and made stains all over the decks, which no amount
of holystoning could remove.

It is a curious fact that it is very rare to find a man
risen from the ranks who can maintain discipline
without a bludgeon or a belaying pin.

This, I think, is due to a lack of sympathy and
insight.   The bucko had no interest in his men over
and above that of the slave driver.   The Westerner
used to say: "No good Indian but a dead Indian."
The bucko looked at his crowd from the same standpoint
—as malingerers out to cheat the ship, as criminals out
to defeat him at all costs, as inefficients to be made
efficient by sheer force of will and strength of fist.

Some people may argue that the bucko mate is the

modern counterpart of the buccaneer and the pirate.
But this is not the case.   The bucko was a hard working
and faithful servant of his owners.   He never let them
down.   He carried on the ship's work with no thought
of self, and, if he adopted the methods of the cave man,
it was chiefly the fault of his education and bringing up;
and his owners and captains were as responsible as he
was for his hard reputation.

The Manning of the Packets.

Before the advent of the steamers, the packets
were well-manned and even in the fifties this continued.
The old *Henry Clay*, for instance, had a complement of
captain, 4 mates, carpenter, cook, steward, 30 seamen
and 2 boys, whereas the *Plymouth Rock* in the seventies
once left Gravesend with 20 foremast hands, not one of
whom could steer and but very few of whom had ever
been to sea before.   And it was wonderful what the
ideal bucko mate could do with such material.   Forty-
two days later, when the *Plymouth Rock* reached New
York, her mate had turned this gang of hoodlums into
very fair seamen, all of whom steered sufficiently well
to satisfy his critical eye.   It is true that in order to
gain this effect the rule had to be "all hands on deck
from daylight to dark."

In the last days of the packets, their officers were
preyed upon by the shyster lawyer of New York.   This
blood-sucker would get hold of the crew of a ship on her
arrival and make them swear to ill-treatment; he then
cunningly waited before serving his warrant until the

ship was about to sail, so that the officer against whom it was sworn either had to pay up the hush money, which, needless to say, reached no sailor's pocket, or else go ashore and lose his berth.

Packet-Rats.

The occupants of Western Ocean foc's'les were divided into two classes. The first of these was peculiar to the trans-Atlantic trade. Its members shipped by the run and rejoiced in the title of "packet-rats." They were, with little doubt, the roughest and toughest customers that ever sailed the seas. Year in and year out they stuck to the packet ships and left them only to die. A full-fledged packet-rat possessed a pride all his own. It was not the pride of a fine seaman, that peculiar hall-mark of the sea, denoting a self-confidence born of resource and capability; but it was the pride of the elemental male in his power to stand hardships and hard knocks. And where only a man of most unusual grit could hope to stay with the life, these packetarians gloried in the very hardness of their service. To be a veteran packet-rat, therefore, argued the possession of a ticket of manhood. Many an old "Western Ocean traveller's" proudest boast was that he sailed in "any man's ship," meaning that no lumping bucko of a mate with fists of iron and a devil's heart could daunt him. And the man who had trained himself to be callously indifferent to either belaying pin, persuader, or knuckle duster was not likely to waste much thought on mere weather conditions. Even in

the mid-winter passage a packet-rat despised clothes
and contented himself with ragged dungarees and cotton
jumpers. He proudly called it "flying light" to come
aboard with only the rags he stood up in, without
blankets, donkey's-breakfast or even oilskins. And
when these rags began to fall off him from hard usage,
he would carelessly rifle the bag of some unfortunate
"joskin." Yet he was not above giving that same
joskin his philosophy of life in the shape of well-meant
advice.

The following is a good specimen of this philosophy.
It was written by a packet-rat himself:—

"When yer git a lick from anny of 'em, officers or men,
jest put it in yer pipe an' smoke it, an' sez you, 'Be
Cripes ! I 'm not killed yet annyway.'"   And here he
shows his pride of race, so scornfully domineering in
the case of the Angle-Saxon.   "For Gawd's sake, pitch
inter the hash an' never let a Dutchman dip in ahead
of ye."

However it must be confessed that if the packet-rat
despised foreign seamen, he equally despised the "deep
water" sailors, especially Britishers—"limejuicers,"
as he disdainfully called them. Here, though, the
proud Western Ocean traveller despised a better man
than himself, as many a rough and tumble between
the rival factions in the streets of Liverpool proved
only too well.

Joskins and Raynecks.

The other class which shared the foc's'le with
the packet-rat was that of the shanghaied landsmen,

the unfortunate greenhorns, known in the packet ships by the queer names of "joskin" and "rayneck," both words of American origin. "Rayneck" or "reyneck," as it was often spelt, I take to be "raw neck," and it may be that "joskin" is derived from "joker."

These miserable "raynecks" were generally boys of eighteen or twenty, who had wandered into the American seaports straight from the plough tail, with perhaps some hazy notion of seeing the world. Naturally they went first of all to the waterfront to see the ships, where they were immediately recognised by the prowling crimps as their legitimate prey. Indeed their gaping mouths and astonished eyes gave them away, even if the traditionary wisp of straw happened to be absent from the hair. Flattered by being spoken to, still more flattered when a drink was offered, they were easy victims. And when later they had the drugged whisky booted out of their fuddled heads by the bucko mate of an outward bound packet, there was little consolation in the thought that they were at any rate seeing the world. This shanghai-ing of greenhorns was chiefly resorted to on the American side, for, strange to say, Americans, who make such prime seamen, do not hear the "call of salt water" as much as other nations, and American seamen have always been scarce except in the Down East fishing ports.

The Liverpool Crimps.

In Liverpool, on the contrary, the crimps had no difficulty in finding men eager to go to sea without the necessary drug beforehand.   The trouble in Liverpool for the crimps lay in the fact that the captains expected able seamen, not ploughboys.   Yet able seamen who knew their worth would seldom consent to ship on the packets.   In those days of real sailormen, an old shellback, before shipping for a voyage, would overhaul every vessel in the docks, sum up her points with care and note every sort of obscure index to her character and that of her officers.   If she was a wet ship, if she carried a taut hand as mate or a slacker, if she was a heavy working ship or an easy working ship;   he knew it at once after one careful scrutiny alow and aloft.   For the position of a chafing mat, a frayed ratlin or a worn brace-block told him volumes, and he well knew the significance of cotton canvas and white decks.

Paddy West's Methods.

Thus the Liverpool crimps found themselves compelled to palm off landsmen on the Yankee skippers. The methods of one of the best known, Paddy West, are told in a famous chanty:

> As I was walking down Great Howard Street,
> I walked into Paddy West's house.
> He gave me a plate of American hash
> And swore it was English scouse.
> Says he, " Come here, young fellow,
> For now you're just in time
> To go away in a clipper ship
> And very soon you'll sign."

Having given him a taste of sea-hash, he next puts him into a sailor's jumper.   The tyro was then ready for the bucket of salt water, which was upset over him by Paddy's cook, a certain notorious Mrs. Waters. This was the "cold nor-wester" in the old chorus.

> Put on your dungaree jacket
>   And give the boys a rest,
> And think of the cold nor'-wester
>   You had down at Paddy West's.

A huge bullock's horn was next placed on the table, and round this the budding sailor had to walk three times. Then, indeed, his deep water experience was complete; he was in a position to say that he had eaten sea-fare, had had the spray of a cold nor'-wester down his back, and had been three times round the horn. It was a simple little comedy, and one can hardly imagine a gimlet-eyed Yankee ever being taken in by it.

Packetarians Well Fed.

There was one great point in which the packets excelled all other ships, and that was in the food served out to the men. The foc's'le "hard tack" on American ships was of better quality than the cabin biscuit on British ships: fresh meat, also, was given twice a week, soft bread every day and potatoes *ad lib.*, not to speak of burgoo, molasses and pickles.

The Emigrants.

With all the ill-treatment that fell to their lot and all the hardships which they had to face, the crew were not those most to be pitied aboard a packet. When the ships were westward bound, they very often carried as many as five or six hundred emigrants in the 'tween decks, and the sufferings of these wretched people can hardly be imagined.

Here are the written words of an old packet captain:—

"These emigrants were the rakings and scrapings of all Europe.   Men, women and children were tumbled into the 'tween decks together, dirty, saucy, ignorant and breeding the most loathsome of creeping things. The stench, below decks, aggravated by the sea sickness and the ship's poor equipment for the work, placed us far below the civilisation of the dark ages.   It was not uncommon in mid-winter to be 50 or 60 days making the homeward passage.   In gales, which were frequent, hatches had to be battened down and *men, women and children screamed all night in terror*.   Ship fever, small-pox and other contagious diseases were common, and it is a wonder that so many survived the voyage as really did.   Rations were served out once a week in accordance with the British Government allowance—just enough to keep starvation away, the estimated cost to feed them being 20 cents a head per day.   The steerage passenger rates were £4."

Steerage rates varied slightly from year to year. In 1842 they were £5 a head, whilst in 1851 during the height of the emigration to America they were only £3 10s. from Liverpool to New York, and about 5s. less to Quebec by the little Allan Line clippers.

In the early days of the packet service, the emigrants were mostly Germans and Irish with a sprinkling of Italians.   Herman Melville gives the following characteristic account of these German emigrants embarking at Liverpool:—

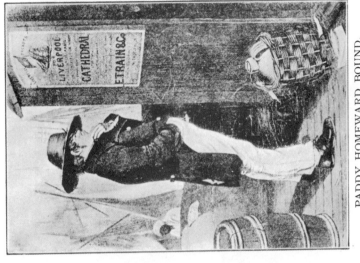

PADDY OUTWARD BOUND
On the Quay of Liverpool.

PADDY HOMEWARD BOUND.
On the Quay of Boston.

"ROSCIUS."

From a Lithograph in possession of the Author.

"There was hardly anything I witnessed in the docks that interested me more than the German emigrants, who come on board the large New York ships several days before their sailing, to make everything comfortable ere starting. Old men, tottering with age, and little infants in arms; laughing girls in bright-buttoned bodices, and astute middle-aged men with pictured pipes in their mouths would be seen mingling together in crowds of five, six and seven or eight hundred in one ship.

"Every evening these countrymen of Luther and Melancthon gathered on the forecastle to sing and pray. And it was exalting to listen to their fine ringing anthems, reverberating among the crowded shipping and rebounding from the lofty walls of the docks. Shut your eyes, and you would think you were in a cathedral. They keep up this custom at sea; and every night, in the dog watch, sing the songs of Zion to the roll of the great ocean organ: a pious custom of a devout race, who thus send over their hallelujahs before them as they hie to the land of the stranger."

The Irish emigrants were as numerous, but very different in their ways. Harum-scarum and happy-go-lucky, they made no preparations beforehand; indeed most of them had an idea that America was only two or three days' sail from Liverpool, and often when the coast of Ireland was sighted after perhaps several days of head wind, they crowded to the rail under the impression that they were looking at the coast of the promised land, and, when told, would hardly believe that it was old Ireland, which they had only left a few weeks before.

These Irish set out for America in their national knee-breeches and swallow-tail coats, often the only clothes they possessed; and also with the most slender store of provisions consisting almost entirely of oatmeal, their staple food being porridge, day in and day out.

In the early days fire and water were the only things found by the ship. The emigrants had to cook their own food at a little galley in the waist of the ship; this galley was hemmed in by the cow-house, sheep, pig and poultry pens and still further circumscribed by the spare spars. It was geneially open to the weather, a mere range of fires, above which a rail with sliding hooks served to suspend the cook pots over the flames.

The sleeping accommodation in the steerage was naturally of the roughest description, often merely shelves of unplaned wood, hastily put together at the last moment by the ship's carpenter. And though the height under the deck beams was seldom more than 6 feet, these bunks were always laid in three tiers. The alleyways between the bunks, often barely 3 feet wide, were blocked up with the kit bags and chests, and also, in the earlier ships, with the private provisions of the emigrants, which took up no small amount of room. In the Black X ships, for instance, every passenger had to show his proper quantity of biscuit, flour, potatoes, tea, sugar and treacle, besides two hams, a tin pot, frying pan, mug, teapot, knife, fork and spoon before being allowed on board. These were usually supplied on the spot by a well-known ship-chandler of Wapping. To pass fore and aft through the 'tween decks, one had to crawl over this litter, and be stopped in one's passage at intervals, either by a baby in convulsions or perhaps a fainting woman or, worse still, a drunken quarrel amongst the men. Steerage stewards were of course unknown. The blind had to lead the blind.

The two busiest men in the ship were the doctor and the carpenter. Chips was perhaps the most responsible person in the ship. He served out the allowance of water and fuel; and his care alone saved the ship from being set on fire time and again by overturned lamps or careless smokers. He was also the ship's dentist.

Port holes, when there were any, were usually set too low to allow of them being opened in a seaway—and being constantly awash gave very little light. Indeed, midway between the companion hatches, the 'tween decks must have been as dark and gloomy as the bottomless pit, the dull flicker of two or three horn lanterns, slung from the beams, being scarcely able to penetrate the foul, fever-ladened air. The only ventilators were a windsail at either hatch when the weather was fine enough.

In spite of all these horrors, the birth rate among the emigrants generally exceeded the death rate.

Epidemics on Packet Ships.

In certain years the death rate from epidemics was very heavy. One of the worst of these was 1853.

The *Washington* arrived at New York from Liverpool in October, 1853, with cholera raging on board. Nearly 100 emigrants had died during the passage, and there were over 60 cases on board when she arrived.

Of other ships arriving that autumn, the *William Tapscott* had 65 deaths; the *American Union* 80; the *Centurion* 42; the *Calhoun* 54; the *Corinthian*, from Havre, 41; the *Statesman*, from Antwerp, 25; the *Delaware*, from Bremen, 15; and the *Gottenburg*, from Hamburg, 27 deaths.

The Emigration Boom from Europe.

At this date the emigration traffic was booming, every nation in Europe supplying its quota. Lindsey gives the following statistics. Between 1815 and 1854, inclusive, 4,116,958 passengers left the British ports; of these 2,446,802 emigrated between 1846 and 1854, and 1,358,096 between 1850 and 1854. In 1854 the new settlers in the States actually remitted £1,730,000 to their relations at home, in order that they might come out to them.

In the late forties and early fifties both the United States and British Governments passed strict emigration laws. In the Parliamentary scale of 1848 each adult passenger had to be issued with the following per week: —water, 21 quarts; biscuits, 2½ lbs.; wheaten flour, 1 lb.; oatmeal, 5 lbs.; rice, 2 lbs.; molasses, 2 lbs.; with potatoes as a substitute for either rice or oatmeal.

At the same time height of 'tween decks and superficial space per passenger were laid down by both countries. Yet in spite of every regulation the lot of the packet ship emigrant was seldom a happy one—and in bad weather it was misery.

Fearful Weather in the Winter of 1852-3; "Roscius" in Trouble.

One of the worst winters in the history of the packets was that of 1852-3. Here is a newspaper account which will give a good idea of the sufferings of the emigrants on the *Roscius* during that winter:—

"The *Roscius*, which left Liverpool on the 17th December, arrived at New York on the 6th instant (6th February). On the 1st of January in lat. 53° 20', long. 28° 50', while under three close-reefed topsails, storm staysails, main spencer and a double spanker, during a strong gale from the N.N.W., she was boarded by a tremendous sea that stove in the upper deck and fore hatches on the maindeck, twisted the mainmast head off and filled the between decks with 4 feet of water. All the stores, provisions and clothes of the steerage passengers were much damaged by this inundation, and no doubt a great part entirely destroyed, as their boxes were washing about the decks until the ship could be brought to and the wreck cleared.

"When that was accomplished, it was found that four of the crew had been washed overboard, the mate had one of his arms broken and one of the crew a leg smashed, besides several of the others severely injured. From the time the vessel left Liverpool until she arrived in port she had to contend against continuous head winds."

At about the same date the *Antarctic*, a fine packet built for Zerega & Co. of New York by Donald McKay, put in to Hampton Roads after a very severe passage from Liverpool, with the added horror of 60 deaths in the ship from smallpox.

The *Lady Franklin*, which left Liverpool on 3rd December, 1852, arrived at New York at the same time as the *Roscius* after an equally stormy trip. On the 7th December she lost a seaman, washed off the bowsprit and drowned. On the 17th she shipped a tremendous sea, which "stove the starboard quarter boats, bulwarks, skylights and binnacle, and injured most of the men, some of them severely. She lost a whole suit of sails blown out of the gaskets in that same instant. Whilst bending new sails at 8 a.m. the same day, two of her hands fell from the fore topsail yard to the deck and were picked up dead."

The toll of deaths on the packets this winter was indeed a severe one, and almost entirely due to the bad weather. The *Patrick Henry* arrived out from London, having lost two of her hands, whilst the *Splendid*, from Havre, reached New York with the loss of seven passengers.

The *Mary Annah*, from Havre, took 88 days on the passage, whilst the *Celestial Empire*, from Liverpool, after a passage of 60 days, arrived New York with the loss of one of her crew and 10 passengers.

Cabin Passengers.

In the first class or cabin, as it was called, seldom more than 25 passengers could be accommodated.

Though they perhaps grumbled louder than the miserable emigrants, they had not much really to complain about; and it is doubtful if the luxurious modern traveller with his beef tea at eleven, French chef, pink and white ices, hothouse fruit, etc., etc., gains half the benefit from a voyage that they did. There was a darkey steward to wait on them, sometimes two, and very often a stewardess.

Christmas Dinner aboard the "Cornelius Grinnell."

The following amusing description in verse of a Christmas dinner aboard the *Cornelius Grinnell* in 1858 gives us a very good idea of the usual cabin fare.

First of all we had some soup, and it was very good,
But as I could not take it, I left it for those who could.
The next course was boiled codfish, and boiled potatoes too,
But that I do not like, so I left it for those who do.
The next course was a stunner, which I must try to relate,
But I could not get a little of each dish upon my plate.
We had a fine roast turkey, just as fine and good
As if you'd just gone and shot it on the prairie or the wood,
A fine dish of stewed chicken, a fine macaroni pie,
Roast and boiled potatoes, and mashed turnips by the bye,
And very good fresh bread, which the steward bakes each day,
Besides sea biscuits, pickles and such fixings in that way.
And when we all had had enough, and that good course was done,
On came the fine plum pudding, and then commenced the fun.
Mr. Clark had brought champagne for himself or for his wife,
And it certainly was some of the best I ever tasted in my life.
He brought it for sea sickness, but they did not drink it on the way,
And he thought we could not do better than drink it on Christmas day.

This feast was served at 2.30, and, with every dish carved or helped on the table, it took about two hours to consume. It was the one great effort of the day on the part of the ship's cook.

There was no dinner, only a sort of high tea, with cold meats perhaps at seven o'clock. Then at the nine o'clock cabin breakfast, porridge and molasses or treacle were followed by the usual dish of dry hash and perhaps topped off with a couple of slices of ham. At 11 a.m. there was no doubt a glass of port or a cocktail to be had, and the usual sardines on toast the last thing at night. During the day there were deck games and card playing, and invariably dancing on fine nights, to be followed probably by songs and the punch bowl. Of course the American national card game, poker, was very much in evidence; indeed, the Yankee packets claim the very doubtful honour of having introduced that most delightful method of losing money into England. Be this as it may, it is very certain that many a staid John Bull was given instruction in the game aboard the packets, paying, no doubt, the usual heavy price for each lesson to the usual polite Southerner or bland New Yorker.

Cabin Passage Rates.

A cabin passage in a packet ship in the forties and fifties usually cost £25 without wine, as against 38 guineas and 1 guinea (steward's fee) charged by the early Cunarders. As competition grew keener and the number of ships increased, these rates gradually fell back to about £20.

Stowaways.

There was still another class of traveller who was fairly numerous. This was the stowaway. If discovered in time he was put aboard the pilot boat or a handy fishing smack, but, if not, he was made to work his passage, after first being terrified out of his life by a pretended hanging at the yard-arm or walking the plank.

Sometimes the stowaway was a woman, in which case there was usually a lover or husband somewhere in the background. Then, if she was pretty and pleaded her cause well, she often succeeded in softening the stubborn heart of the hard packet captain and so gained her ends.

Captain Urquhart's Vigia.

During the whole of their existence the American sailing packets were unusually free from disaster or shipwreck, but when the steamers first appeared on the Atlantic breakdowns of machinery, collisions with icebergs and other ships and a host of minor troubles were more than frequent. More than once a packet had the satisfactory duty of carrying the passengers of a helpless steamer to their destination. Perhaps the most tragic as well as most curious of these cases was the rescue of the survivors of the *Ville de Havre* by the *Trimountain*. The story, as told by Captain Urquhart, of *Trimountain*, is especially interesting, for the chain of circumstances which led him straight to the scene of the tragedy can only be explained by the single word "Providence."

In the winter of 1868, the *Good Hope*, Captain Urquhart's ship, lay in the Shadwell Basin, London Docks. It was the custom of the packet captains when in port together to dine with each other in rotation on

their respective ships.   It happened one evening that
Captain Urquhart was entertaining Captain Robinson
of the *Patrick Henry*, and Captains Champion and
Larrabee.   The talk came round to "vigias," and
Captain Robinson declared that he had seen the rock
"Barenetha," reported by the sailing ship *Crompton* in
1807.   This rock, though frequently searched for, had
never been sighted again, yet Captain Robinson declared
stoutly that he had not only sighted it, but taken two
good observations at the time, and, if they would go
aboard his ship, he promised to show them its exact
position on the chart.

Robinson had the reputation of being very imagin-
ative, so neither Champion nor Larrabee treated his
statement seriously.   Larrabee was a man celebrated
on the Atlantic for his wit, and the chaff flew thick
round Robinson's head, and he was told that his rock
was either a dead whale or a wreck bottom up.   However, Captain Urquhart's curiosity was aroused in spite
of the others' chaff, and the sight of the rock, clearly
marked down on Robinson's chart, so impressed him
that he carefully pricked off the fabled "Barenetha"
on his own chart.

Providence did not show its hand again for five years.
In November, 1873, Captain Urquhart was in command
of the *Trimountain*, then loading in New York.   The
stevedores finished work late on a Saturday afternoon.
As is the case with most owners, the *Trimountain's*
expected his captain to get away early on Sunday
morning.   But to this the captain strongly objected,

HURRICANE OFF LIVERPOOL,
JANUARY 7 AND 8, 1839. Loss of *Pennsylvania*, *St. Andrew*, and *Victoria*, packet ships,
and *Lockwoods*, emigrant ship.

Painted by Samuel Walters.
From the MacPherson Collection.

Published by Henry Lacey.
Drawn on stone by T. Fairband.

"CORNELIUS GRINNELL."

From the MacPherson Collection.

urging that he had never left port on a Sunday if he could avoid it, and declared that he would not be responsible for the success of the voyage if the owner insisted. The latter, though very surprised, gave in to the captain's scruples and the ship did not sail till Monday.

The third coincidence or act of Providence was Urquhart's resolve to set a more northerly course than usual. It was purely an experiment on his part; being the off-season for icebergs, he had no fear of that danger and so decided to see if the shorter distance to be sailed would make up for the loss of the favourable Gulf Stream current.

The fourth coincidence was the miscalculation of the charterers in engaging freight, so that 70 feet of the upper 'tween decks were left vacant, the ship being already down to her marks. This space was constantly looked over by Captain Urquhart with the idea of its convenience in case he came across a broken down passenger steamer, and he even calculated the number of people he could put there. The passage was uneventful as far as the Banks of Newfoundland, where the ship was wrapped in fog for several days.

How the Survivors of the "Ville de Havre"- "Loch Earn" Collision were rescued by the "Trimountain."

I will now quote Captain Urquhart:

"About 10 o'clock on the evening of 21st November, the fog cleared and the stars were shining brightly. An hour or two later I got two observations of the

Polar star, computed my latitude and found my longitude by dead reckoning. Having crossed the Atlantic many times, I seldom looked at the general chart, for I knew my way from New York to England as well as I did from the Battery to Harlem; but being now north of my usual track I thought I would prick her off on the chart. I found to my surprise that if my reckoning was correct, we were going straight for Barenetha's Rock, and only a few miles away. I began to be considerably disturbed. I went on deck. There was no moon, but the stars were still shining brightly. I looked on both sides of the ship and ahead; and said to myself, "A light could be seen a long distance to-night, but we will be right on to a rock, unless it be a very large one, before the course could be changed." I did not remember what Robinson said about the size of the rock. 'Oh, what nonsense,' said I, 'Robinson never saw a rock! What a fool I am! No other man of sense would be bothering about a rock that does not exist!'

"So I gave the course, east by south, to the officer on deck, told him to let me know if there was any particular alteration in the wind or weather, and lay down on the lounge, with the compass over my head, to sleep.

"Looking at the compass, I said, 'East by south—right straight for Barenetha's Rock! Confound the rock! What a chump I was to go aboard Robinson's ship and take the location of a rock from a yarn-spinner like Captain Robinson. Captains Champion and Larrabee of our party paid no attention to it. I am a coward— I'll just go to sleep anyhow!'

"I turned my eye to the compass again and still found myself repeating:—'East by south—right straight for Barenetha's Rock!' I turned over on my side and said I would keep my eyes off the compass: and then shifted back with eyes closed—but there was no sleep for me. I took another look at the compass but the same thing occurred. 'Well,' said I, 'I guess I'll look at the chart again.' The dot within the circle seemed bigger than ever. But what had that to do with it? thought I.

"It got to be nearly one o'clock in the morning, when I went on deck again. The chief officer, who had the watch, was a much older man than I and had always been in the North Atlantic trade. I finally, though much ashamed, asked him, after a few minutes' conversation about the watch, if he had ever heard of any one who had seen any of the rocks laid down on the charts 50 or 100 years ago.

"He ridiculed the idea; and said that he had travelled many years in this trade, and had never seen a rock or heard of anyone who had. I felt a little more composed and went back to the lounge, and tried again to sleep, but it was the same old thing. I looked at the chart once more; and then the ship gave a tremendous lurch to port.

"'My God!' thought I. 'She's struck the rock!'

"I hurried to the deck to learn that it was only a sea larger than the others which she had tumbled into; but I made up my mind then and there that I would be tormented no longer, so I said to Mr. Pool, the chief officer:—' We are rather north of our usual track and the wind is nearly dead aft. Keep her up two points S.E. by E. until daylight. It'll make the sails draw better and give her more speed.'

"What a relief the changing of the course was !

"I went to the lounge and slept like a child until I was called by the second officer at daylight, who reported that there was a disabled sailing ship four points on the starboard bow."

I have quoted this in full, as, although there have been many yarns of this description, where the captain is generally besought by a mysterious voice or even a mysterious writing on the log-slate to steer a certain course, here is a real instance of this curious working of Providence.

If Captain Urquhart had not altered his course when he did, he would have missed the disabled sailing ship, which proved to have been in collision with the passenger steamer *Ville de Havre*. The tragedy is a well-known one. The two ships collided for no apparent reason, at least it was never satisfactorily cleared up, and the *Ville de Havre* carried 200 souls down with her. The sailing ship, which was an iron Scotchman, the *Loch Earn*, was only saved by her collision bulkhead and by being in ballast, and she managed to save 85 of the *Ville de Havre's* people by her boats. These were transferred to the *Trimountain* and safely conveyed to Cardiff. The crew of the *Loch Earn* tried to get her to port, but in vain. After terrible sufferings they were taken off by a smack and landed on the coast of Ireland after nearly perishing from exposure and furious weather. If the *Trimountain* had not been so curiously directed to the scene, it is certain that the 85 survivors from the *Ville de Havre* must have been lost, for the tiny smack could not have accommodated them.

Conclusion.

The packet ships have passed away with their steel nerved skippers, bucko mates and devil-may-care crews. The Western Ocean Traveller is no more. Sail has given way to steam and petrol—the art of sea craft to the cunning of machinery—the virility of a hard life to the comfort of a soft life. And are we the better for it? Is this the right way of civilisation and progress or will this complex, mechanically-ridden world have to return to the simpler, more robust life, after some cataclysm which will shatter machine-made force, or some scientific discovery in the realms of electricity and magnetism, which will drive the steam engine and its coal sack, the combustion engine and its oil can into the scrap-heap?

Let us hope it may be so, and that the arm which pulls a lever may once more grow muscle in fisting a sail: and the hand that turns a wheel or sets a pointer may regain its grip on the handle of a plough and the round of a rope, and its touch on the driving rein and the tiller.

We should all be the fitter, the happier and better if we could return to the wide horizons of land and sea, to nature and the simple life, and face away from the foul aired towns and soul destroying factories.

APPENDIX

APPENDIX I.

Abstract Log of the Ship "Garrick,"
Captain R. W. Foster, from New York to Liverpool and
from Liverpool to New York, 1854.
(From "Maury's Sailing Directions.")

REMARKS ON THE "GARRICK," BY CAPTAIN FOSTER.

The *Garrick* was built at New York in the year 1836 under the superintendence of E. K. Collins. Her futtocks, apron and stern frame consists chiefly of live oak and locust of great dimensions, as is also her floor timbers. The whole of the frame is placed closer together than is usual in merchant ships.

Her tonnage is 895$\frac{56}{100}$ reg., and sailing qualities fair for a full built ship. She has performed a great deal of hard service, and in all probability is capable of doing so for some years to come. She has, however, in common with the other three ships of the Dramatic Line, been most shamefully neglected and allowed to go to destruction in hull and rigging.

This was well exemplified on the recent winter's passage from Liverpool, when rigging, block strops, etc., constantly came tumbling about our heads and the hull was as leaky as a sieve.

FROM NEW YORK TO LIVERPOOL.

Cargo.—Cotton, lard, naval stores, corn, wheat, manilla, hemp, flour and American cotton canvas.

Passengers.—Second cabin—49 adults principally English from Illinois and Michigan. Several of these, females chiefly, are afflicted with fever and ague.

May 10.—A.M. departed from Staaten Island. At noon passed Sandy Hook.

May 11.—Noon, lat. 39° 45′ N., long. 69° 00′ W. Wind S. by E., under full sail. 8 p.m., sharp lightnings in the S.W., N.W. and northern quarters. Threatening, shortened sail, to accomplish which had great difficulty owing to the inefficiency of the crew. Delightful weather, ocean smooth, many peterels in our wake. Saw Gulf or tropical weed. Distance run 203 miles.

May 12.—Noon, lat. 39° 36′ N., long. 66° 20′ W. Wind south to
S.S.E. light, rate 4 knots, strong current rips. Weather pleasant,
ocean smooth. A little before dusk passed through extensive streams
of Gulf and rock weed, tending S.S.E. and N.N.W. A solitary whale
seen. Water these 24 hours continuing very green. Stormy peterels
in the wake. Steered by compass so as to make a E. ½ N. course.
Course S. 85° E., 129 miles.

May 13.—Noon, lat. 40° 5′ N., long. 63° 21′ W. Winds 2 to 5 a.m.
calm, then E.S.E. to S.E. and east, rate 1, 3, and 4 knots. Pleasant
though sultry. About 4 p.m. the water from a deep green changed to a
greenish blue. A moderate swell from S.S.E. Rock and Gulf weed,
wilted grass and straws. After the moon arose a more beautiful lunar
atmosphere I never beheld. 6 to 9 a.m., a quick short undulation from
south, a moderate swell from E.S.E. Passed during the forenoon a
nautilus under swelling sail and with pliant oars, also a very singular
looking mollusk, red as a lobster with 5 or 6 blunt projections and as
large as a middle sized turtle. When in the stream, the agitation of the
current was quick and fine, water 71° of a deep ocean blue. When at
7 bells we emerged, water 68°, the colour became a bluish green.
Course true E. by N. ½ N. Distance, including current, 134 miles.
No peterels seen since yesterday afternoon.

May 14.—Noon, lat. 39° 31′ N., long. 62° 27′ W. Wind E.S.E.,
east, to E.S.E. rate, 3, 4, 5 knots. Consigned to the care of Neptune
a well-corked bottle containing a paper to ascertain the currents of
the ocean. 2 and 3 p.m., passed Gulf and rock weed, straws and
circular mollusca. Water quite green, a school of porpoises to the eastward. A dense fogbank to the northward, 4° to 5° above the horizon.
It has the appearance of distant land. A solitary pair of peterels in the
wake. Ocean this afternoon literally impregnated with mollusca, also
a numerous species, which have the appearance of the blue bottle fly.
Great quantities of weed, wilted grass, straws and fish spawn. 5 p.m.,
tacked to the S. by E. A species of mackerel, called by sailors "skip
jacks," playing near the ship. Sunset clear, a golden yellow sky,
a flock of gannets about. All last night and this morning strong
scents of wilted seaweed, such as we often smell on the seashore.
Noon, tacked to the northward and eastward. Course S. 56° E.
Distance 62 miles.

May 15.—Lat. 39° 51′ N., long. 59° 34′ W. We have been in the
Gulf Stream greater part of the 24 hours. 2.15 p.m., water fell to 66,
the colour of a bluish green. Tacked to southward. The fog is still
seen to the N. and E. 6 p.m., tacked to eastward. A delightful morning.
Large quantities of Gulf weed. Ocean impregnated with animalculæ,
the sparkling blue marine insect numerous. A gentle swell from the
east. Course N. 81½ E. Distance 133 miles.

May 16.—Lat. 40° 58′ N., long. 56° 24′ W.   Wind S.E. to south, rate 3½, 2, 1.   We begin to feel the swell from the E.N.E.   We have had the advantage of the stream the whole 24 hours.   A deep blue tint with gentle ripplings.   Course N. 65 E.   Distance 159 miles.

May 17.—Lat. 42° 1′ N., long. 55° 4′ W.   Wind catspaws, E.N.E. to S.S.E., rate 0 to 2.   A fleet congregated, some of which I recognised as having sailed three or four days before us.   Swell continued from E.N.E.   At 9.30 p.m. the Aurora Borealis commenced, colour a yellowish white light, not intense, principal coruscation and shooting at right angles with the horizon, 15 to 20, and in direct line to Polaris. By half-past ten the Aurora had dispersed.   Ocean impregnated with animalculæ and numbers of the sparkling blue insect.   On examining a tumbler of this sea water with the sextant microscope (a powerful one) they appear of all shapes, some contending, avoiding and in pursuit, others in steady rapid motion, and some dormant.   Like-wise a species of mollusca serpent, contracting and expanding, 9 inches in length, of a deep red from the head to about 3 inches down the body.   The tumbler of water after remaining half an hour exposed to the sun's rays, life became extinct.   Course N.E. by E.   Distance 72 miles.

May 18.—Lat. 42° 18′ N., long. 54° 40′ W.   Wind N.N.E. to S.W. doldrums, rate 0 to 2 knots.   Calm with indications of a continuance. A fogbank to northward.   A school of fish 1½ inch in length alongside. Numerous peterels, they utter a sort of shrill double chirp, especially in the night time.   A light swell from W.S.W. and east.   Delightful summer weather.   Course N. 29 E.   Distance 20 miles.   Consigned to the care of Neptune a bottle with usual directions.

May 19.—Lat. 41° 26′ N., long. 53° 43′ W.   Wind east to N.E. rate 5. A school of porpoises going to S.W.   Swell from W.S.W., S.E. and E.N.E.   At 4 p.m. a smart breeze to northward of us.   Two vessels came up at the rate of 5 miles per hour, the wind being N.N.E.   Our ship lay becalmed within ½ mile of the breeze.   From 5 to 8 p.m. breeze alternately S.W., N.E., N., S. and east.   Strong ripplings, current apparently setting to N. and E.   Little or no weed.   At 10.30 entered the stream.   Rock and Gulf weed, kelp, some wood with barnacles on it, water deep indigo blue.   Stormy peterels about.   Course S. 41 E. Distance 69 miles.

May 20.—Lat. 40° 6′ N., long. 50° 57′ W.   Winds east, E. by S. 6½ to 5, the lower scud flying rapidly to the S.W. and whirling round in circles, fine, white and fleecy.   A continued high S.E. and E.N.E. sea. Noon tacked to northward.   Saw yesterday afternoon two ships bound to the westward ; from being in this parallel, I infer they must have encountered ice far south of the homeward track.

May 21.—Lat. 40° 32′ N., long. 48° 50′ W.   Wind E. by S. to E.N.E.

5 knots. At 3.30 p.m. temperature of water lowered from 68 to 62, a bluish green; saw a large iceberg bearing north distant 12 or 14 miles. I am confident that it is the melting of this berg and perhaps others that gives the water so green a tint. 4 p.m., tacked to S. by E. in anticipation of the wind veering to S.E. 4.30, passed the junction of green and blue waters. Ripplings like small breakers, we now encounter a short chop of a sea and the ripplings of the current seemed like broken water. At about 20 minutes to 6 the wind veered suddenly from S.E. blowing strong; tacked ship to E.N.E. I now built my hopes on a good run to northward and eastward, when about 7 p.m. we emerged from the stream into green water and to my disappointment the wind veered to E. by S. and moderated. Ocean became smooth and we entered a chilly atmosphere. 10 p.m., a faint flash of lightning to eastward. 12 p.m., tacked to S. and E. At 5 a.m. in the stream unsettled squally weather with a ruffled sea. Wind veering S.E. Tacked to E.N.E., after running into green water, wind veered to east, moderated and the weather seemed settled. 10 a.m., a fogbank to northward. 10.25, entered it. Water 44. At 7 bells tacked to S.E. Water 46. Course N. 75 E. Distance 99 miles.

May 22.—Lat. 40° 54′ N., long. 47° 49′ W. Wind E.S.E. 6, 5 knots. 5 p.m., saw a whale sporting. At 7.20 p.m. entered into current of the stream; the margin appeared like broken water and we immediately encountered a heavy S.E. sea into which our ship pitched the bowsprit. Commenced to shorten sail, but before we had succeeded, lost the jib. Such a crew of lubbers is enough to make the heart sick, 18 in number, 10 of whom cannot discriminate between the stem and the stern, and only 4 out of the remaining 8 can steer. By 10.30 p.m. the wind settled to a double-reefed topsail breeze. 12 p.m., wore ship to the N.E. Course N. 64 E. Distance 54 miles.

May 23.—Lat. 42° 23′ N., long. 47° 38′ W. Wind E.S.E. 5 knots. Numerous stormy peterels. 6.30 p.m., wind E. by N. tacked to southward and eastward. A high sea from S.S.E. to E.S.E. Ship pitching heavily. 5 a.m., tacked to N.E. At 10.15 a.m. saw an iceberg bearing N.N.W. distant 10 miles, 25 to 30 feet high. Strong current rips. Course N. 5 E. Distance 90 miles. Invariably more settled when to the north of the stream.

May 24.—Lat. 43° 19′ N., long. 46° 58′ W. Winds E.N.E. to E.S.E. 5 to 4 knots. A tumbling swell from S.S.E. Towards evening wind fell almost to calm and veering E.N.E. tacked to southward and eastward. 7 a.m., tacked to N.E. No Gulf weed seen. Peterels in the wake. Course N. 31 E. Distance 66 miles.

May 25.—Lat. 44° 4′ N., long. 46° 33′ W. Wind E.S.E. to east 3 to 3½ knots. 7 bells, tacked ship to S.S.E. A continued S.S.W. swell, quick not high. 4 a.m., tacked to N.E. Delightful weather. A large school of black fish and porpoises.   Course N. 22 E.   Distance 51 miles.

May 26.—Lat. 45° 6′ N., long. 46° 38′ W.   Wind E.S.E. to east. 3½ knots.   Continued swell from S.S.W., also from E.N.E., long and rolling.   Saw this afternoon a large shark, also a right whale, nearly ahead of our ship, lying on its side with one fin and one fluke of the tail out of the water.   This animal was either sick or wounded as it manifested much uneasiness.   Our ship ran against it which seemed to take it by surprise.   It sank with considerable effort and after getting astern came to the surface and resumed its former position of body.   7.30 a.m., tacked to S.S.E.   Course true N. 87 W.   Distance 63 miles.   Heading up N.E. and N.E. ½ N. on starboard tack and S.S.E. on port tack.

May 27.—Lat. 44° 3′ N., long. 45° 56′ W.   Wind E.S.E. to S.E. 2 to calm, then S.S.E.   Ocean smooth, swell from N.E. and S.S.W.   Clear close to the western horizon, all other parts overcast.   Sunset in an eclipse forming a crescent.   11 a.m., saw a ship to southward with a southerly wind, sails full.   At 11.30 a light breeze from S.S.E.   Course S.S.E.   Distance 69 miles.

May 28.—Lat. 44° 31′ N., long. 44° 56′ W.   Wind S.W. southerly to calm 3 to 0.   From indications given by throwing over a ball of wet ashes, the current on surface sets S. and S.E.   I have frequently seen this tried on a voyage to India but never had much faith in its correctness.   In some measure I think it may be depended upon.   Wood ash is the best.   Ocean smooth, bluish green, with swell from eastward. Many nautilus, much rock weed, little Gulf weed.   Course N. 60 E. 56 miles.   Saw a piece of wood thickly covered with barnacles; also two large sharks.

May 29.—Lat. 45° 27′ N., long. 41° 32′ W.   Wind S.S.W. to S.W. by S. 3 to 5 knots.   A school of black fish going to the N.W.   Saw a diver. Passed much rock weed.   Nautilus and 2 sharks alongside.   Very pleasant weather.   Course N. 69 E.   Distance 155 miles.   A very large shark passed close to the ship.

May 30.—Lat. 46° 39′ N., long. 37° 13′ W.   Wind S. by E. 5 knots. Ocean smooth, weather delightful.   Saw a large whale lashing the water.   Saw another large shark.   Ocean very smooth without any perceptible swell, a very uncommon occurrence in this part of the Atlantic.   Course N. 72 E.   Distance 197 miles.

May 31.—Lat. 48° 20′ N., long. 33° 38′ W.   (D.R.).   No more stormy peterels seen.   A copious dew, the lofty sails saturated.   We passed yesterday two vessels bound to the westward with studding sail booms rigged out on the starboard side.   Gloomy looking to the eastward.   Course N. 62 E.   Distance 181 miles.   Threw over a well corked, sealed and wired bottle with usual request.   No more weed seen. I continue daily to observe molluscæ and medusæ, many of which differ from others as the ship's position on the ocean is changed.

June 1.—Lat. 50° 9′ N., long. 31° 7′ W. Wind E.S.E. to S.S.E. 5 knots. Strong current rips. Towards evening easterly swell increased. 6 a.m., there must be bottom here at a few hundred fathoms, water being the colour of a very light green such as we often see in shoal soundings. 9 a.m., sky clearer. Colour of water beautiful light peagreen. 10.30, water gradually darkened to indigo blue. Swell from E.S.E., N.E. and N.W. great current rips. Course N. 40 E. Distance 143 miles.

June 2.—Lat. 50° 40′ N., long. 30° 34′ W. Wind east 3 to 0. A little before 1 p.m. we again entered into water of a peagreen resembling the colour over the Bahama Banks and imparting to the sky a deep purple tint. Threw over a bottle. 3 a.m., stood to the S.S.E. 8 a.m., to the N.E. Course N. 34 E. Distance 38 miles.

June 3.—Lat. 51° 11′ N., long. 29° 27′ W. Wind east to S.E. 2 to 3 knots. A swell from the E.N.E., N.N.E. and westward. Appearances indicate a northerly wind. Mercury falling, swell increasing and atmosphere cooling. Surely we must have a change. 6 p.m., tacked to southward. Until 12 p.m. wind veered from east to S.E. by S. 12, tacked to northward and eastward. Wind veering to S.E. A rolling swell from E.S.E. and E.N.E. Weather pleasant. Course N. 59 E. Distance 61 miles. Threw over a well corked and copper wired bottle.

June 4.—Lat. 52° 4′ N., long. 26° 15′ W. Wind S. by E. ½ E. to S.S.E. 4. Swell from east increasing. A large flock of grey gulls hovering around for last few days. Aurora commenced about 12 p.m., not vivid. Delightful weather. Course N. 66 E. Distance 130 miles.

June 5.—Lat. 53° 13′ N., long. 21° 20′ W. Wind S. by E. to south, 4. Ocean a beautiful bluish green. Weather pleasant. A moderate swell from eastward. Five ships in company, the *Garrick* outsailing three, one outsailing the fleet. By 7 a.m. the fast ship within 2 miles astern. The ship proves to be the *Washington* from New York. By 10 alongside she now holds a better wind but cannot forereach the *Garrick*; another ship astern overhauling us. Wind astern fresher and more southerly. Course N. 69 E. Distance 189 miles.

June 6.—Lat. 53° 20′ N., long. 20° 46′ W. Wind S.E. to S.S.E., 4 to 1. Wind getting light, an undulation from S.S.W. The wind a short distance astern probably from that quarter. Ocean smooth. About 4 p.m. a swell commenced rolling along from W.N.W. which by 8 increased to a considerable height. The sunset clear in a splendid golden yellow sky. With the *Washington* and the other ship, the *Henry Clay*, we have sailed side by side up to the present time. 8 p.m., a sail ahead, raising her pretty fast. Westerly swell heavy. 9 a.m., ships continue side by side. Mercury rising with unusual rapidity.

10.30 a.m., 30° 27', delightful weather. Course N. 68 E. Distance 23 miles. A solitary black fish appearing alongside, fired into it, after which it was no longer seen.

June 7.—Lat. 53° 29' N., long. 20° 8' W. Wind S.S.W. to S.S.W. and S.W by S. 0 to 3. Considerable swell from W.S.W. 2 p.m., the ocean alive with animated matter. A school of fish, from 1 to 1½ inch in length, under the counter and keeping pace with the ship. Presently a solitary fish, about 4 inches in length, darts amongst them scattering the school in all directions. Course E. by N. ½ N. Distance 27 miles. One sail ahead, a new clipper ship, overhauling her fast; by 4 p.m. up with her. The other ships in company. Should the wind continue from the southern quarter, I will decide to pass through the North Channel.

June 8.—Lat. 54° 2', long. 16° 19' W. Wind S.W. by W. moderate. Studding sails alow and aloft. Six sail in company this afternoon, three hauling up for Cape Clear. 4 a.m., *Washington* and *Henry Clay* ahead, hull down. Meridian, *Washington* out of sight. Hold our own with the *Henry Clay*. Consigned to the ocean a bottle well corked. Saw a large whale this morning going north.

June 9.—Lat. 54° 52' N., long. 12° 26' W. Wind S.W. by W., 5½ to 7½ knots, then N.W. and W.N.W. fresh, with moderate squalls. Overcast sky. Both ships have left us out of sight. 6 p.m., sighted a vessel ahead. A swell rolling from N.W. 6 a.m., nearly up with the sail, a bark. Course N. 73 E. Distance 170 miles. Passed to Neptune another bottle.

June 10.—Tory Island, N. 80° E., distant 147 miles. Water green. 2 a.m., saw the N.W. point of Ireland. 9 a.m., Tory Island bore south distant 8 miles. Current last 24 hours set strong to southward. Weather pleasant. Numerous large whales sporting round the ship.

June 11.—At 3 p.m., passed Inishtrahull, inner passage. The *Washington* and *Henry Clay* passed here this morning. We were boarded by a boat from the island. Exchanged or bartered for fish, potatoes, eggs and milk. Nine families besides the lighthouse keeper's are located on the island. It contains in a pleasant little valley 9 acres of arable land. There are also numerous little patches of verdure, enclosed naturally by basaltic crags, which afford grass for the cattle. These, in winter, are conveyed to the mainland. At noon between the mouth of Cantire and Glenarm Bay. This channel is an ugly place in a gale.

June 12.—Wintry looking weather. The rain has ceased. Mercury, 4 p.m., 29. 9/100. Wind S.S.W. blowing a double reefed topsail breeze. Mercury, 6 p.m., 29. 7/100. Heavy gales. Rathlin Island West 7 miles. 7 p.m., wind veered to W.S.W., a fine looking sky to N.W. Mercury rose to 29.16. Wind veering to S.W. and S.S.W., light and blowing in gusts.   7 a.m., passed near to the reef of rocks called the Maidens.   At noon Copeland Island West 9 miles.   Will dodge under its lee, until next flood.   Weather pleasant.   Wind in offing south to S.S.W.   In shore S.S.W. to S.W. single reefs, topgallant sails over. The *Washington* and *Henry Clay* in sight from the Isle of Muck yesterday morning.   During the night strong gales from S.S.W. and heavy rain split the fore topsail and outer jib.   Re-bent others.   I expected to see the old foresail go next.

June 13.—Squally at intervals.   1 p.m., two smart squalls of wind, hail and rain.   Squalls generally caused the wind to veer to W.S.W. 2 p.m., passed near to Copeland Island.   Ship gaining southing fast against a strong ebb.   1.40 a.m., South Rock Light bore west.   Tacked to the southward and eastward.   Wintry looking weather at times. 4 a.m., tacked to westward.   11 a.m., tacked to S.E.   South Rock Lighthouse N.W. 7 miles.   Noon, squally with rain, veering the wind to W.S.W.   Hope to weather the Calf of Man.

June 14.—Squally and gloomy looking weather.   3 p.m., tacked to the N.W.   At 6, South Rock Lightship bore N. by E. distant 10 miles.   Tacked to southward, wind for the first time since we entered the Channel west.   12 p.m., lights on the Calf of Man in range.   5 a.m., received a pilot off Point Linas.   10.30 a.m., anchored in the port of Liverpool.   So ends this tedious passage.   Met the *Washington* off the bar.   The *Henry Clay* arrived last evening.

LIVERPOOL TO NEW YORK.

Cargo.—395 tons iron, 59 tons steel.   This latter is stowed amidships, forward of the centre of the hold.   The former is distributed on the coal, fore and aft, from the foremast to the mizenmast and both affect the compasses seriously.   The rest of the cargo consists of tin, coal, dry goods, casks and crates.

Passengers.—Emigrants—English 86, Scotch 14, Irish 324, other countries 11—total 435.

July 3.—4 p.m., passed Rock Lighthouse.   Much rain, wind W.S.W., blowing heavy.   8 p.m., wind W.N.W., dark gloomy, wintry looking weather.

July 4.—Wind moderating.   4 a.m., tacked off the Isle of Man to the southward and westward.   At noon off Holyhead.   Weather pleasant, atmosphere clearing, wind N.W. by W.

July 5.—Wind light varying from W. to W.N.W.   10 p.m., N.W. moderate.   9 a.m., Tuscar bore W. by N. distant 6 miles.   At noon a strong breeze came from N.N.W.   Saltees N.W. 14 miles.

July 6.—Lat. 50° 28′ N., long. 8° 42′ W.   Wind north to N.N.W., rate 5 knots.   A swell from west.   Weather pleasant.   Ocean indigo blue.   Course S. 46 W.   Distance 122 miles.

July 7.—Lat. 49° 0′ N., long. 12° 17′ W. Wind north by W. to north, 6 knots. Passed a corked bottle. A high irregular sea. Ship easy.* Course S. 61 W. Distance 185 miles. Water lightish green.

July 8.—Lat. 47° 50′ N., long. 16° 39′ W. Wind N.N.W., north to N. by E., 5 to 4½ knots. A high irregular sea, gloomy looking weather. 8 p.m., a school of porpoises keeping pace with the ship. Passed this forenoon a singular looking mollusca, large as a 20-gallon keg. Ocean smooth, water a bluish green. Course S. 65 W. 167 miles. Local attraction affecting the compasses not less than 1½ points. I much regret not being in possession of an azimuth compass. To purchase one for the ship would be considered as an extravagance, not to be pardoned. It is a common idea with mates in these ships that westerly variation is greater in going to the westward than in going to the eastward, without reference to the iron cargoes.

July 9.—Lat. 47° 8′ (D.R.), long. 20° 00′ D.R. Winds N.N.E. to N. ½ W., 5 knots. A pair of peterels in the wake. The ship stirred up in the wake this evening immense quantities of mollusca, large as an onion and of a red purple hue. Water light green and smooth. Course W. by S. ½ S. Distance 144 miles. Consigned to Neptune a well-corked and copper wired bottle with the usual request to transmit, etc.

July 10.—Lat. 46ᶜ 51′ N., long. 24° 19′ W. Wind N.E., 5 to 6 knots. Weather pleasant. A high swell from west and N.E. Passed this forenoon a branch of kelp 6 to 7 feet in length with many barnacles on one end, also rock weed. Course W. ½ S. Distance 179 miles.

July 11.—Lat. 46° 56′ N., long. 25° 9′ W. N.E. wind falling calm. Passed this afternoon a bale of cotton having barnacles on it, also a large log covered with barnacles. A cross swell from S.W., W., N.E. Ocean impregnated with animalculæ, also numerous mollusca of a beautiful red and brown. The surface of the ocean exhibited a species of mollusca enclosed in a brittle membrane. two of these I send to Lieut. Maury. Course W.¾ N. Distance 38 miles.

July 12.—Lat. 48° 13′ N., long. 25° 31′ W. Wind north to N.W., 2 to 5 knots. A high swell from N.E. and from the westward. 12 p.m., tacked ship to the W.N.W., wind hauling westerly. 6 a.m., tacked to the N.N.E. Latter part ocean smooth, colour indigo blue. Very strong current ripplings this forenoon. Course N. 24 W. Distance 57 miles.

July 13.—Lat. 49° 29′ (D.R.)., long. 24° 48′ (D.R.). Wind N.W. to north 5 to 6, whole sail. A swell rising from the westward. 5 a.m.,

* Comparatively so. A law has been enacted, limiting emigrant ships to a certain weight of cargo and draught of water. An excellent law, as ships were overburdened with iron cargoes and deadweight.

tacked to the W.N.W.   A few minutes before 4 o'clock a.m. passed near to a space of very light green water, about the dimensions of the ship not so wide.   The officer of the deck became alarmed and ordered the helm to be put hard a-weather to avoid it.   This spot could not have been reflected by the sky, as at the time there was a dense· mist. Course N. 34 W.   Distance 90 miles.

July 14.—Lat. 49° 50′ N., long. 27° 55′ W.   Wind north to N.W., 5 to 4.   Early part of the evening Aurora faint, 11 p.m., tacked to N.N.E.   7 a.m., tacked to W.S.W.   10.30., stood to N. by E. ½ E. Weather pleasant.   Course N. 64 W.   Distance 48 miles.

July 15.—Lat. 50° 7′ (D.R.), long. 29° 31′ (D.R.)   Wind west to N.W.   Strong gales.   Weather unsettled.   At midnight wind veered suddenly W.N.W.   A very high and irregular sea.   Ship under double reefed topsails and reefed courses.   Water deep blue.   Course N. 65 W. Distance 64 miles.

July 16.—Lat. 47° 51′, long. 30° 20′.   N.N.W. gales to N. by W. more moderate.   Strong gales, sea high and irregular.   Passed vessels bound to the eastward under close-reefed topsail.   A.M., weather pleasant, under full sail.   Course S. 13 W.   Distance 136 miles.

July 17.—Lat. 48° 8′ (D.R.), long. 31° 28′ (D.R.).   Towards evening the wind began to fall.   8.30 p.m., breezing up from the westward and backing against the sun, a sure indication here of unsettled weather. I have long fully appreciated the value of the barometer.   From 5.30 to 8 a.m., heavy rains, the wind blowing in violent gusts.   From 8 until 10, apparently settled, mercury sinking fast.   At 11 the gale began to increase, close reefed the topsails and veered ship to S.S.W. At noon a heavy gale W.N.W.   Ship under close-reefed main topsail and storm fore and aft sails.   Course N. 69 W.   Distance 49 miles.

July 18.—Lat. 48° 30′, long. 32° 44′.   Heavy gales, sea running high especially from west, round to N.W.   Towards evening moderating. A high irregular sea.   Latter part swell N.N.E. to S.E.   Passed poly-pusses.   Weather apparently unsettled.   Heavy condensing air flew to the N. and W.   The lower strata seem to proceed from fogs.   Course S. 30 W.   Distance 113 miles.

July 19.—Lat. 46° 27′, long. 33° 21′.   Wind W.N.W., N.W. by W. 5 knots. 8 p.m., tacked ship to the northward.   1.30 a.m., tacked to the S.W.   8 a.m., tacked to N. by E.   Weather pleasant though apparently unsettled.   A swell from N.N.W.   Passed sprigs of rock weed.   Course S. 84 W.   Distance 27 miles.

July 20.—Lat. 46° 56′ (D.R.), long. 34° 50′ (D.R.).   Wind W.S.W. to south and calms.   Weather apparently pleasant though appearances in the atmosphere indicate an unsettled state or commotion.   Heard to-night the shrill sharp chirp of the peterel.   Great quantities of rock weed sprigs. Course N. 64 W. Distance 68 miles. Threw overboard a bottle with ship's position with usual request if found to forward to Lieut. M. F. Maury, U.S.N.

July 21.—Lat. 46° 32′, long. 38° 7′. Wind N.N.E. to N.E. by N., 6 to 3 knots. Weather unsettled, indicative of a change. Much rock weed. Passed a large log, one end of which had been sawed. At 3.45 the breeze came from E.N.E., blowing fresh with rain. 5, mercury began to rise. A heavy westerly swell, strong winds. Towards sundown moderating. All sail. Passed this morning a 3-inch plank. Numerous sprigs of rock weed and one piece of Gulf weed, quite fresh. Weather very pleasant. Course S. 79 W. Distance 137 miles.

July 22.—Lat. 46° 6′, (D.R.), long. 39° 36′ (D.R.). Wind east to S.E. to S.W., 3, 2, 5 knots. Weather pleasant, an irregular swell from N.E. and west. Great quantities of a singular looking mollusc, 1 to 4 feet in length and 4 to 5 inches in breadth. Many in coils, serrated parts deep red, other parts yellow and green. Also greyish coloured serpents, some 6 feet in length, contracting and expanding. Procured a part of one of the former for Lieut. Maury.* Latter part atmosphere unsettled. Course S. 68 W. Distance 87 miles.

July 23.—Lat. 45° 16′, long. 41° 21′. Wind S.W. by W. to N.N.W. At 11 p.m. wind veered to N.N.W. 4 a.m., a dense fogbank in the south. The lower strata of clouds proceed from dense fogs in the N.W. quarter. Course S. 86 W. Distance 90 miles.

July 24.—Lat. 44° 07′ (D.R.), long. 44° 56′. Wind north, strong at intervals. Wintry looking weather. A high swell from the northward. Rock weed and peterels. Course S. 60 W. Distance 168 miles.

July 25.—Lat. 44° 11′, long. 46° 52′. Wind N.N.E. to N.N.W., calm, catspaws. A tumbling swell from northward and eastward. No rock weed seen, many tufts of Gulf weed, polypusses and mollusca. Many peterels. Course N. 87 W. Distance 84 miles.

July 26.—Lat. 44° 39′ (D.R.), long. 48° 53′ (D.R.). Calm, S.S.W. to S.E. A tedious time. Passed this morning a monster mollusc of the same species we saw on the 22nd inst, fully 10 feet in length and a foot in breadth. A school of bottle-nosed whales sporting around the ship. Transparency of water 36 feet. Course W. by N. 60 miles.

July 27.—Lat. 43° 55′, long. 49° 12′. Wind N.N.E., calm, E.N.E. to west. 3 p.m., a faint breeze came from the N.N.E. Immense quantities of sea fowl feathers passed from 5 p.m. until dark, through continued collections. Ship going 4 miles per hour. From 5 to 12 p.m. almost calm below, all sails aloft, clean full. Several large whales playing round the ship. In 55 fathoms very white sand. Position too

---

* By sinking a small cord some fell across it, but invariably were cut in two parts. Ocean literally alive with them.

far west, current the preceding 24 hours must have set to the northward and eastward.

July 28.—Lat. 43° 43′, long. 52° 6′.   Calm to S.W. by S.   Many large whales sporting.   3 p.m., the breeze sprang up from S.W.   Passed a schooner at anchor.   Current setting to the northward.   Course true up to 6.30 p.m., west 16 miles.   Temperature of water from 54 changed to 59.   A gentle undulation from the westward.   Ocean smooth. Passed a binnacle with a brass top to it.   Strong current rips.   Course S. 84 W.   Distance 126 miles.

July 29.—Lat. 42° 55′, long. 56° 15′.   2 p.m., wind veering westerly. A high westerly swell commences.   Current rips strong.   Sultry, indicative of a change.   8 p.m., the wind veered or came from north. Passed this forenoon a large square stick of timber, some rock weed, abundance of Gulf weed.   Weather delightful.   Course S. 75 W. Distance 189 miles.

July 30.—Lat. 43° 9′, long. 55° 20′.   North, N.W. by W., calms· 6 p.m., tacked to N. by E.   Aurora Borealis faint.   Ocean smooth.

July 31.—Lat. 42° 29′, long. 57° 6′.   Wind S.S.W., 4 knots.   Entered into a heavy westerly sea.   A beautiful aerial sunset scene.   Very sultry, nimbus gathering in the N.W.   Course N. 75 W.   Distance 79 miles.

August 1.—Lat. 42° 00′, long. 58° 55′.   Wind N.N.W. to N. by W. Shortened sail, much lightning and heavy rains at intervals.   Wind flying from north to S.W.   3 p.m., wind S.W. by S.   Calm with a heavy S.W. by S. sea.   8 p.m., the wind came from N.W.   In the stream, much Gulf weed.   Course S. 60 W.   Distance 98 miles.

August 2.—Lat. 41° 41′, long. 61° 15′.   N.N.W. to calm to W.S.W. A continued head or westerly sea.   Towards evening abating.   At 5 a.m., a breeze sprang up from W.S.W.   Much Gulf weed.   Weather pleasant.   Course——.   Distance 120 miles.   This day a female child was born of English parentage.   It is named Virginia Garrick Brown.   A land bird alighted on board, species unknown.

August 3.—Lat. 42° 29′, long. 62° 30′.   Wind W.S.W., west, calm, W.N.W.   Saw a flying fish.   4 p.m., emerged from the stream, powerful current rips.   After leaving the stream entered into a westerly sea. 9 p.m., much lightning in S.W. and west quarters, also in N.E.   A heavy shower of rain.   A heavy W.S.W. sea.   Latter part strong current ripplings.   Westerly sea subsides.   Course N. 50 W.   Distance 74 miles.   Caught a land bird with yellow breast.

August 4.—Lat. 41° 56′, long. 63° 00′.   Wind west moderate.   2.30 p.m., tacked ship to the northward.   8 p.m., tacked to S. and W.   Power- ful current rips appear at times like broken water.   A westerly swell. At 9.20 a.m., entered the stream.   Tacked to the N.N.W.   Much

Gulf and rock weed on the edge of the stream.   A dense fogbank in the northern quarter.   Notwithstanding the powerful current ripplings which have prevailed these 24 hours, the ship has made no more westing than the courses and distances have given.   I therefore am inclined to believe that there has been a regular flux and reflux of the ocean tides.

August 5.—Lat. 41° 58', long. 64° 40' (D.R.)   Wind calm, S.E. to N.E. moderate.   Ocean exceedingly agitated by current rips.   Water greenish blue.   At 9 a.m. wind came suddenly from N.E.   Course by compass N. 78 W.   85 miles.   True S. 67 W. 85 miles.   Suppose the current to set S.S.W.

August 6.—Lat. 41° 14', long. 66° 16'.   Wind N.E. to N.N.W. Passed this afternoon much wilted grass.   Ocean smooth.   Passed this forenoon green grass, straws, pieces of wood, chips, much rock weed and other substances.   Calm below, a light breeze aloft.   Course S. 46 W.   Distance 63 miles.

August 7.—Lat. 41° 9', long. 68° 5'.   At 5 bells p.m. entered into the stream.   Water 70.   Tacked to N.N.W. and shortly the water fell to 64.   When we entered the stream the atmosphere cleared immediately, after the water falling to 64, foggy.   At 6.30 a.m. sounded in 22 fathoms.   Tacked to the southward.   Weather pleasant, atmosphere a little hazy.   Ocean smooth.   In 28 fathoms, coarse sand, yellow, black and white gravel.

August. 8.—At 6 p.m. saw a pilot boat to the westward.   At 10.30 p.m. received a pilot.   Wind E.N.E. faint.   11 a.m., N.N.E. 2.

August 9.—First part light winds from N.E. by E.   Part of the middle part calm.   Latter part, wind strong from E.N.E.   Lat. 40° 9', long. 71° 34'.   A strong southerly current.   7 p.m., passed Fire Island. 10 p.m., saw the Highland lights.

Early in the morning of the 10th arrived at the city.

APPENDIX II.

Voyage of the "Jamestown." Commander R. B. Forbes.

One of the quickest voyages ever made between Boston and the British Isles was that of the U.S. sloop-of-war *Jamestown*, which the celebrated Captain R. B. Forbes raced across to Ireland with a cargo of food stuffs, contributed by the ever charitable Americans towards the relief of the Irish famine of 1847, the *Jamestown* being lent by Congress for the purpose.   The sloop began to load at Boston on St. Patrick's Day and sailed for Cork on 28th March, 1847.

Captain R. B. Forbes, who was her volunteer commander for the voyage, was a retired sea captain and a well-known Boston shipowner. He ranks as one of the foremost men in the great days of American shipping, and on the New England seaboard his memory is still green.

I give the voyage in the captain's own words taken from a rare little pamphlet of memories, which he published in his old age.

At about 8 a.m. on March 28th, the gallant ship was at the end of the wharf, with topsails set, topgallant sails sheeted home, the courses and spanker in the brails, the jib ready to hoist, the fasts had been singled, and all was ready to cast off, when the bowfast parted, and as her head swung off the sternfast was let go, the jib and the topgallant sails were set and we waved adieu to a crowd assembled on the dock, one of whom, my old friend Commodore James Armstrong, said he came to see the last of us.

While we were preparing to start, he appeared alongside with a lugubrious countenance, and when I asked as to the cause, he spoke something to the following effect : " I am sorry to see you going off at this season in that deeply laden ship with such a short crew; what are you going to do when it comes to getting up anchors?"   I answered that that was something I had not taken into consideration. " I don't expect to let them go before arrival at the Cove of Cork where I can procure help to raise them, and as to being deep, if she was a merchant ship and was not more fully laden I would turn out my captain."

After passing Fort Independence, it flashed across my mind that my trusty friend and cousin, Joseph Lyman, who had shipped as my private secretary, had not appeared.   The tug was close on our port quarter and I hailed her and requested them to go back and get him, but the request had scarcely reached them when I annulled it. I felt very averse to losing a single hour of that fine north-west breeze.

Arriving outside of Boston Light about 10.30 a.m., I was asked to heave to for the purpose of putting out Mr. Phillips, our pilot. I declined to do so and told the captain of the tug to come up close to the port quarter: this being done, we put the pilot into a bowline in the port spanker vang, and landed him on the forecastle of the tug.

The members of the committee and the crew gave us three hearty cheers, and we went on our way rejoicing.

We took our departure from the Highlands of Cape Cod at 3 p.m., the fine breeze held on long enough for us to clear George's Shoals, when the wind came out at north with snow and sleet, when our new and stiff hemp ropes became as hard as crowbars, and our rather short crew almost as stiff.

I must pause to give a short account of the condition of the good ship. She had recently been fitted with new lower rigging, leaving the old back stays: all the gun deck ports had been planked up, and all but two of the guns taken out: new running rigging had been rove: the launch, with a cutter stowed in her, was placed on the gun deck, and the large grating hatch well secured: every space below the gun deck including water tanks, ward room and storehouses, was filled with provisions, excepting a small place chock aft accessible by a scuttle in my cabin, where it was important to get at the tiller and wheel ropes, which worked on the ward room deck, and a small place in the main hatch, where the cable compressors or brakes worked: the pumps still delivered their water on the gun deck—a good deal got in at first at the hawse holes and much more at the rudder port, so that we soon found it necessary to jog the pumps every watch. In order to get rid of the young Niagara entering at the rudder port, we bored holes so as to let the water into the hold.

The first night out we washed away the quarter gallery deadlights, where, as well as at the stern ports, which had not been caulked in, there entered a good deal of water, rendering my cabin very wet and uncomfortable.

March 29.—Wind moderate at west-north-west to north. Thermometer 28 on deck and 38 in my cabin. Set all studding sails, made 198 knots. Lat. 42° 34′, long. 65° 31′.

The number of effective men to go aloft, including one mate, 31; sick, lame and blind 4.

In view of the heavy ropes and canvas, I ordered a snug reef in the big mainsail, and much of the time we had single reefs in the topsails, with topgallant sails over them, all of which would have been unnecessary had the ship been rigged after my plan.*

---

* Forbes's double topsail rig.

There were many ropes unknown to our experiences, such as clew and bunt tackles, boom jiggers, rolling tackles and burtons: there were four heavy tackles at the lower mastheads, which, by the way, we found use for in setting up the lower rigging several times. The topsail sheets and tyes were of raw hide; in short, there were many ropes which were encumbrances. We lost no time in reeving suitable tacks and sheets, cutting off royal tyes and sending down many things which we did not require. The boatswain, who had served in men-of-war, thought we were mad.

March 30.—The wind came out east-south-east, decks full of snow and sleet, thermometer 28. Midnight, wind hauled to N.E. by E., we came up to E.S.E., going 9½ knots pretty close to the wind under topgallant sails, and she makes the water fly, but is quite stiff enough.

March 31.—Light winds at N.W., part of the day nearly calm. In the morning the wind came out at S.E., at 8 a.m. going 9 knots, heading about E.N.E. Thermometer 33 in the water. 4 p.m., reefed the topgallant sails. At 5 p.m. single-reefed the topsails, ship came up to east, a thick fog, fresh flaws and large sea getting up. At the end of the day strong breezes and threatening weather: took in the reefed topgallant sails, and put another reef in the topsails and spanker, ship going 8 and 9 knots and jumping like an antelope. Lat. 42° 37′, long. 59° 28′.

April 1.—Fresh gales at S. by E. and a large sea. Morning made more sail, going 9 knots close at it. fog dense ; the wind seems to be nailed between S.S.E. and S.E. by E. Ends strong breeze at S.E. Lat. by D.R. 43° 26′, long. 55° 4′.

April 2.—During the night the fog turned to hard rain, with symptoms of a gale: the sky black as Erebus: called all hands at 11 p.m.; furled the mainsail, and by 1.30 a.m. got the ship snug. During the middle part the wind came out at W.S.W. with snow squalls: every rope as stiff as in January. Thermometer—air 32, water 33. The third mate reports seeing appearances of ice just before daylight. At noon lat. 43° 13′, long. 51° 18′.

Necessity being the mother of invention, I devised a method of partially warming my cabin, by suspending a grapnel and keeping on it four 32 lbs. shot heated in the galley. The floor of the cabin was kept wet by water oozing in through the stern ports and the quarter galleries.

April 3.—At 1 p.m. the weather cleared up somewhat and the sea going down, made all sail to the eastward. At 6 p.m. sounded in 45 fathoms. Middle and latter parts the wind was baffling between south and S.E.; the thermometer in the air 31 and in the water 29 to 32. Latter part going 7½ knots close-hauled. Lat. 43° 32′, long. 50° 24′.

Sunday, April 4.—Commences with a fresh breeze at S.E. and

foggy; going 9 and 9½ close-hauled, with light sails in, heading E. ½ N., and all hands on the alert ready for tacking. At 7 a.m. ship heading E. by S., going 10½ to 11 knots, with the wind one point free. In the morning the temperature of the air changed several degrees, and the water from 32 to 37. At noon the air was 48, a thick fog. Lat. 45° 04′, long. 46° 52′.

April 5.—Fresh gale at south, ship going 11 to 12 knots. At 2 p.m. furled topgallant sails and single-reefed the topsails and spanker. In the evening the wind canted S.S.W. Uncle Sam's hide ropes do not stand like chains. At 10 p.m. weather threatening; called all hands and got snug by 1 a.m.; reefed down to three-reefed fore and main topsails, whole foresail, spencer and reefed spanker ; split the fore topmast staysail and saved the jib with difficulty. After keeping about S.E. to get the canvas snug, we bore away to E.N.E., a large sea running and the tops occasionally coming over forward of the main rigging: the ship steers beautifully, and could not be easier in her motion. In the early morning the wind moderated; were obliged to haul up to keep her steady, and swiftered in the lower rigging until it could be set up carefully. Lat. 46° 21′, long. 42° 43′. Made 195 miles.

April 6.—Begins with a fresh breeze at N.E., with dark rainy weather. At 9 p.m. took in royals and flying jib. At 10 took in topgallant sails, the old swell under our lee prevents our carrying all the sail we wish: at 7 a.m. the wind came out at S.W.: from 8 to noon ship going 11 to 11½ under single-reefed topsails; reefed mainsail; a large sea rising; the fore truss got adrift, secured it without damage. Lat. by D.R. 46° 24′, long. 39° 15′.

April 7.—Commencing with a strong breeze at S.W.: at 4 p.m. set the fore topmast studding sail: at 5 going 12 knots; parted more of the green hide sheets and split the main topsail in consequence. Lat. 47° 51′, long. 34° 12′. Made 265 knots. 10 days 3½ hours out.

April 8.—The fine S.W. wind continues, ship going 10½ and 11 easily. This is the first pleasant day since sailing. Lat. 48° 29′, long. 28° 43′. Made 249 knots.

April 9.—First part moderate: evening, ship going 10½ to 11; passed within hail of a ship bound west and received three cheers. Made 245 knots.

April 10.—Wind at W.S.W., ship going 10 to 11. Middle part moderating: speed down to 8 knots, all sail out, including studding sails on both sides. Lat. 49° 30′, long. 18° 30′. Logged only 177.

April 11.—Sunday—two weeks at sea: throughout moderate at W.S.W. to west, all studding sails set on both sides, the weather cloudy and sometimes rainy. Lat. by D.R. 50° 15′, long. 14° 09′. Logged 178.

April 12.—Begins moderate and canting to W.N.W., all sail out going

7 to 8 knots.   At 8.30 came up with and spoke a bark 25 days from Philadelphia bound to Liverpool, we being 14½ from Boston.   At 11 a.m. a fine breeze, going 13 knots with the wind on the port quarter.   Not having had any good observations for several days, we had during the night kept well clear of the land: hauled up as gradually as the sticks would bear to make the land; made it about noon, and hauled up for the Old Head of Kinsale, and ran down for the entrance of Cove of Cork, the wind blowing fresh from W.N.W., double-reefed topsails.   At 2 p.m. took a pilot, who ran into our port quarter gallery and stove it, and as usual with these fellows demanded indemnity in the shape of beef and pork for breaking his rail.   Anchored in the outer harbour at 3.30 p.m.   We have only tacked once since leaving Boston.   While running in with studding sails set and chains bent, enough water came in on the gun deck to float a barrel.   When we came to anchor with the sails not snugly clewed up, the starboard anchor not fetching the ship up, we let go the port anchor, and in snubbing her the stopper in the main hatch was broken, but fortunately we brought up with a good scope out.   Before night we had a visit from Lieutenant Protheroe sent by Admiral Sir Hugh Paget, with a tender of services.

In looking over this record the nautical reader will see that while we did not have a large proportion of fair winds, we had winds enabling us to make good slants, and we took advantage of them by letting the ship go good full, and never doing what too many navigators do, namely, bracing very sharp and bobbing at a head sea.

I do not hesitate to say, that if the *Jamestown* had been properly rigged before starting, and had not laboured under the disadvantage of new lower rigging fitted in cold weather and old backstays, we should probably have saved a day.   And if she had the double topsail rig, I think we should have saved at least two days.

While preparing for sea, I consulted Captain J. C. Delano of New Bedford.   He said that on the last days of March we would sail on the very worst day of the year for England, and if we got to Cork in 30 days we ought to be well satisfied.

An incident of our good fortune, which was mainly due to the vigilance of my officers, Messrs. W. F. Macondray and James D. Farwell, I may mention that the clipper ship *Rainbow*, Captain John Land, left New York a day or two before us, as was proved by laying down her track on my return, was not far from us about the 3rd April, near the tail of the Banks.   Captain Land took the more prudent course of tacking to the southward instead of running across, as we did, in thick weather.   In truth, I felt from the beginning that the *Jamestown* was under the special care of Providence in all things *except the bad rig and the leaks*, and when my officers suggested the danger of running across the Banks in thick weather, I consoled them by referring to that special care, and kept on in fear and anxiety.

When in California in 1870 I met Captain Farwell, and he referred to my remark as to the special care of Providence, and he added "Notwithstanding what Mr. Forbes said about Providence, he made us keep a very sharp lookout and kept all hands on the alert ready for stays."

Having discharged the cargo into Government stores and received about 150 tons of limestone for ballast, I called on the Admiral to express thanks for his very active assistance, whereupon he ordered the *Zephyr* to take us in tow. I asked how far we might take her and he answered, " Just as far as her coal holds out." We started at 3.30 p.m. on the 22nd April and soon made sail; and finding that we were likely to outrun the *Zephyr* we discharged the pilot and cast off the tow rope,

Friday, April 23.—Light airs and calms all day, and we want steam; many vessels in sight which we outsail easily.

April 24.—Head winds and pleasant weather: getting on very slowly.

April 25.—Begins with strong breezes S.W. to W.N.W., latter part a gale, ship under three-reefed topsails, foresail and spencers: the ship making 8 knots close-hauled. At 4 p.m. heading off to the north, wore ship to S.W.

April 26.—From midnight to 6 a.m. moderating: in the forenoon the wind increased until at 3.30 p.m. it blew a hard gale at west and squally: a large sea getting up: the wind inclining to the N.W., wore ship under three-reefed topsails and reefed spencers: during the evening a heavy gale with hard squalls: the ship behaves nobly, and ships no water except sprays. I have not seen such a gale since 1832.

April 27.—To 1.30 p.m. the gale much the same: the ship lies to like a duck, under main topsail: at 2 p.m. a little more moderate, set three-reefed fore topsail: at 5 set fore sail and close-reefed mizen topsail. At 7.30 p.m. squally, gave her the reefed mainsail. In the morning a brig passed bound east, scudding under only a fore topmast staysail; evening squally, the ship going 8 to 8½ knots with a big sea on, and she makes the water fly. I have a good crew and officers. At 10 p.m. came up with and passed close to a large schooner under trysails, in fact lying to. Lat. at noon 49° 52′, long. 18° 50′, only 500 miles on our way and nearly five days at sea.

April 28.—Begins with an increasing breeze: at 1 a.m. took in the mainsail: at 2.30 very squally; a ship passed close to us under short sail, bound east; at 4 a.m. quite a gale again, took in the foresail, mizen topsail and spanker; at 5 very severe squalls; at 6 took in the fore topsail; at 8 more moderate, set it again; at 9 set reefed courses and close-reefed mizen topsail ; at 11.30 squally, up mainsail; at 12 set it again and let a reef out of the fore and mizen topsails: ends squally.

Lat. 47° 45′, long. 19° 23′. To the end of the day less squally, the ship going rapidly and jumping lively under two reefs in topsails, whole courses, spencers, spanker, jib and reefed topgallant sails: broke the main truss and gave Uncle Sam's rigging a good trial.

April 29.—A.M., the wind nearly all gone heading off to the south, tacked to W.N.W., lat. 45° 5′, long. 20° 25′. Evening wind light at W.S.W.

April 30.—First part moderate and pleasant. Wind W.S.W., then squally, took in royals and flying jib occasionally.   P.M., breeze fresh and squally, wind canting, tacked to the W.S.W.   Took in and set reefed topgallant sails occasionally.

May 1.—Begins with a fine breeze at N.W. the ship is going 10 close-hauled.   At 11 a.m. made a sail on the lee bow and at 3.30 p.m. came up with and spoke the packet ship *Baltimore* from Havre, 17th April, bound to New York, 14 days out to our 9.   At 6 p.m. she is hull down astern.   We have not laid our course for an hour since leaving Cove. Lat. 43° 28′, long. 26° 22′.

May 2.—Begins light winds from the westward.   At 1 a.m. tacked to the N.W., wind springing up.   At 6 a.m. the *Baltimore* in sight 4 or 5 miles to leeward; at 10 she was out of sight.   Lat. 43° 12′, long. 28° 12′.   10 days out and no fair wind yet.

May 3.—Wind ahead, middle part strong breeze and squally, from 2 to 3 a.m. reducing sail, ship pitching considerably.   At 3 a.m. John Hughes was lost off the jibboom while furling the jib, at the time the ship was going 10 to 11 knots; the night was very dark and the men who were with him on the boom did not discover he was missing until some time after they came in.   In the evening the wind shifted suddenly from ahead in the S.W. to ahead in the W.N.W. and blew hard in squalls. At the end of the day we are pitching into it under double reefs, going 8 and 9 knots.   Lat. 43° 44′, long 32°.

May 4.—Moderating fast.   At 8 a.m. close-hauled with all sail set going only 4 or 5 knots, ana finally at noon only 3 knots.   Lat. 41° 48′, long. 34° 10′.   In the afternoon squally, took in royals, flying jib and mizen topgallant sail.   At 4 set them again, at 6 took in light sails and reefed the spanker; at 8 p.m. going 9½ heading N.W., breeze freshening, double-reefed the topsails; before midnight the wind increased to a gale, took in third reef in topsails, reefed and furled the mainsail.   We have done more reefing so far than is usually done in a whole China voyage.

May 5.—At 1 a.m. furled the foresail and the mizen topsail; to 3 a.m. headed off to north, wore ship to the S.W.   From 4 to 7 a hard gale, the ship under three reefed topsails, reefed spanker and spencers.   Lat. 41° 20′, long. 36°.

May 6.—1 a.m. a heavy squall, reduced sail; at noon all the reefs are out except a single one in topsails. Lat. 39° 18', long. 38°. At 2 p.m. made all sail to royals and flying jib, ship going 11 knots easily; this is the nearest approach to heading our course since leaving Cove. At 8 p.m. quite moderate, the sails scarcely asleep and she goes 8 knots.

May 7.—Begins light head winds. At 2 p.m. tacked. At 8 heading west going 9 knots. At 10 took in mizen royal, going 10. Lat. 38° 7', long. 40° 31'.

May 8.—Throughout pleasant with a small breeze from N.N.W.; latter part the ship headed her course for the first time since leaving Cove 16 days ago; ship going 7, close-hauled with the sails flapping. At 6.30 set starboard steering sails. The sea very smooth. Lat. 37° 5', long. 44° 35'. Made 196 miles with the sails scarcely asleep.

May 9.—Light variable winds in the western board, the weather dreadfully fine; my patience nearly exhausted   Lat. 36° 42', long. 45° 13'.

May 10.—Moderate and pleasant, the wind W.S.W. going from 8 to 9½ close-hauled. Spoke English brig *Enterprise* from Barbadoes for London. Lat. 38° 12', long. 47° 11'.

May 11.—Begins breezy with a sharp head sea; 2 a.m., took in topgallant sails. At 4 single-reefed topsails. At 5 a.m. set topgallant sails. At 6.30 the wind came out suddenly from the N.N.E., put her head W.N.W. · At 9 going 12½ and waiting for the old sea to subside a little so as to set studding sails. At 10 the wind backed to N. by W. At 10.30 set the royals and starboard studding sails. At 11 cannot go our course, took in studding sails. At 11.30 ship coming up, set them again. At 12 our fine breeze nearly all gone and were obliged to brace up sharp. At 2 p.m. a dead calm. Lat. 39° 29', long. 50° 8'. We have laid our course nearly four hours and have made our studding sails useful only about three hours.

May 12.—Begins calm. At 3 a.m. a light breeze from west, heading N.N.W., going from 5 to 8 knots; weather fine and sea smooth. At 8 a.m. boarded the ship *Virginia* of New York, 27 days from New Orleans, bound to Liverpool; heard of the fall of St. John de Ulloa and Vera Cruz to General Scott. Lat. 39° 54', long. 51° 18'. At 9.30 ship going on her course, a remarkable event.

May 13.—Begins dark and cloudy, ship going 9 to 9½ on her course. In the morning set studding sails, going 11 knots. At 5 a.m. a sail in sight ahead. At 9.30 passed her and read her name *Robert Burton*. At 1 p.m. could just see her by getting on the hammock rail; from 8 a.m. to 8 p.m. going 11 to 13 knots with all light sails set, including studding sails, the wind about east. Lat. 40° 10', long. 54° 40'. Logged 244.

This is the first steady fair wind we have experienced, the ship steers perfectly and rolls easy.

May 14.—Throughout a fresh gale at east with rainy weather at 7.30 the water 38, air 42, sounded but got no bottom.   Since noon the air has changed from 55 to 42 and water from 62 to 38.   Distance made 295.   Lat. by D.R. 41° 40′, long. 60° 35′.

May 15.—First and middle parts fresh gale and rough sea, the ship going like a racehorse under single-reefed topsails and reefed topgallant sails.   The weather foggy and very cold, air 36 to 42, water 36 to 40. In the morning we are approaching the meridian of Cape Sable, but we can only guess at our latitude and so we go on carefully sounding every two hours and getting no bottom, we conclude we are to the south-ward of our reckoning.   At 5 a.m. hauled up to N.W.; at 9.30 the sun shining out dimly.   I took 30 sights and our position was 65° 10′.   At 10 a.m. hearing a cry of "Sail ho! close on board," I jumped on deck and saw a brig standing to the S.E. under double reefs.   I immediately cried out " Hard a-starboard, call all hands," and whipped the good ship around under topgallant sails and came up close under the lee of the brig, and ascertained that she was directly out of St. John's and she reported lat. 42°, long. 65°.

Having thus confirmed the position, we wore round to W.N.W., and before noon it cleared off sufficiently to give us a good latitude, 42° 14′. At 2 p.m. we are going 12 knots with all the muslin spread.   At 5 speed reduced to 11 and at 6 to 10.   During the night the wind was at N.E. and pleasant.   At 6 a.m. made Cape Ann bearing N.W.   At 8.20 took on board from the *Sylph* Mr. Phillips, the same who took us to sea on 28th March.   At 8.50 passed through Hyprocrite Channel, and at 9.30 anchored off the Navy yard.   It was then I realised fully that we had accomplished a remarkable voyage.

APPENDIX III.

—

Some Specification Details of the " Cornelius Grinnell."
(From the Illustrated London News,
August 31, 1850.)

The *Cornelius Grinnell* is built of oak, scantlings mostly of yellow pine. She is seasoned with salt, caulked in the hold and well ventilated. She has 12 inches dead rise at half floor, a foot swell or rounding of sides and about 26 inches sheer.

Her keel is sided 16 inches, moulded 30 inches forward and 26 inches aft; the floor timbers in the throats are 12 inches by 17 inches; she has 3 keelsons, each 15 inches square, or combined 15 inches by 45 inches, making her backbone about $7\frac{1}{2}$ feet through from the top of the keelson to the base of the keel, of course, including the moulding of the floor timbers.

There are two bolts through every floor timber and the keel; one of $1\frac{1}{4}$ inch copper driven through and rivetted, and the other of refined iron of the same size, driven through the keelsons and down blunt into the keel.

She has also sister and bilge keelsons, and a stringer 7 feet below the deck, over which the lower ends of the hanging knees lap and through which they are bolted. The sister keelsons are 15 inches square, bolted through the navel timbers, the midship keelsons and each other. The bilge keelsons, two on each side, are 10 inches by 16 inches, and the stringer is 14 inches by 15 inches, all square bolted with $1\frac{1}{4}$ inch iron.

The ceiling on the floor is $4\frac{1}{2}$ inches thick, square fastened with inch iron, and all the other ceiling up to the deck is $7\frac{1}{2}$ inch thick, also square bolted : in a word she is square fastened throughout. Forward she has 7 hooks and pointers; and aft 5, all of oak and very closely bolted.

About 10 feet above the ceiling she has 7 hold beams, viz., one before the foremast, 3 between it and the mainmast, and 3 between the main and mizen masts. These have standing, lodging and hanging knees of oak, and pass through the midship stanchions, which are fitted to support them and extend to the beams above. These beams are 15 inch by 12 inch; the lower deck beams 15 inch by 16 inch, and the upper deck beams 15 inch by 16 inch, all of southern pine.

The hanging knees of the hold are of oak, those in the 'tween decks of hacmatack; and her hold stanchions, which are 10-inch square, are kneed to beams and keelson. These are entirely new points of construction. The lower deck waterways are 15 inches square, and the two strakes over them 10 by 12 inches, those inside of them each 5 inches by 7 inches, bolted vertically and horizontally. The planking of both decks is $3\frac{1}{2}$ inches thick, and the ceiling of the 'tween decks is all 5 inches except the clamp which is 6 inches. Her transom is 16 inches square, the knees and breast hooks in the 'tween decks are very stout and closely bolted. The upper deck waterways are 12 inches square, the plank sheer 6 by 16 inches, and main rail of same substance. Her garboards are 7 inches thick, the next strake 6 and the third 5 inch, which is tapered to $4\frac{1}{2}$ inches, the substance of the planking at the bottom. She has 20 strakes of wales of 7 by $5\frac{1}{2}$ inches and the waist's is $4\frac{1}{2}$.   Her bulwarks are $5\frac{1}{2}$ feet high and surmounted by a monkey rail.

APPENDIX IV.

Chief Ships built by Donald McKay.

1842	*Courier*	- -	380 tons	(A)	Built at Newburyport.			
1842	*Ashburton*	- -	449 ,,	(A)	,,	,,		
1843	*St. George*	- -	845 ,,	(A)	,,	,,	Packet ship	
,,	*Joshua Bates*	- -			,,	,,	,,	,,
1844	*John R. Skiddy*	-	930 tons	(A)	,,	,,	,,	,,
,,	*Washington Irving,*				Built at Boston		,,	,,
,,	*Anglo-Saxon,*				,,	,,	,,	,,
1846	*New World*	-	- 1400 tons	(A)	,,	,,	,,	,,
1848	*Ocean Monarch*				,,	,,	,,	,,
,,	*Anglo American*	-			,,	,,	,,	,,
1850	*Cornelius Grinnell*	-	1100 tons	(A)	,,	,,	,,	,,
,,	*Staghound*	-	- 1535 ,,	(A)	,,	,,	Clipper ship	
1851	*Daniel Webster*	-	1187 ,,	(A)	,,	,,	Packet	,,
,,	*Staffordshire*	-	1817 ,,	(A)	,,	,,	,,	,,
,,	*Flying Cloud*	-	- 1793 ,,	(A)	,,	,,	Clipper	,,
,,	*Flying Fish*	-	- 1505 ,,	(A)	,,	,,	,,	,,
1852	*Sovereign of the Seas*		2421 ,,	(A)	,,	,,	,,	,,
,,	*Bald Eagle*	-	- 1790 ,,	(A)	,,	,,	,,	,,
,,	*Westward Ho*		- 1650 ,,	(A)	,,	,,	,,	,,
1853	*Star of Empire*	-	2050 ,,	(A)	,,	,,	Packet	,,
,,	*Chariot of Fame*	-	2050 ,,	(A)	,,	,,	,,	,,
			1640 ,,	(Reg.)				
,,	*Empress of the Seas*	(No. 1)	2200 tons	(A)		,,	Clipper	,,
			1647 ,,	(Reg.)				
,,	*Great Republic*	-	4556 ,,	(A)	When launched		,,	,,
			3357 ,,	(A)	,, rebuilt		,,	,,
,,	*Romance of the Seas*		1782 ,,	(A)			,,	,,
,,	*Lightning*	-	- 2084 ,,	(A)	Built at Boston Australian			
			1468 ,,	(Reg.)			packet ship	
1854	*James Baines*	-	- 2525 ,,	(A)	Built at Boston Aust. pkt. ship			
,,	*Champion of the Seas*		2448 ,,	(A)	,,	,,	,,	,,
			1947 ,,	(Reg.)				
1855	*Donald MacKay*	-	2595 ,,	(A)	,,	,,	,,	,,
			2408 ,,	(Reg.)				
,,	*Defender*	-	- 1413 ,,	(A)	,,	,,	Medium clipr.	

1855	*Amos Lawrence*			Built at Boston Medium clipr.			
,,	*Abbot Lawrence*			,,	,,	,,	,,
1856	*Minnehaha*	-	- 1698 tons (A)	,,	,,	,,	,,
,,	*Mastiff*	-	- 1035 ,, (A)	,,	,,	,,	,,
1857	*Alhambra*	-	-	,,	,,	,,	,,

During the Civil War he built several gunboats.

1868	*Helen Morris*	-		Built at Boston Medium clipr.			
,,	*Sovereign of the Seas* (No.2) 1226 tons (Reg.)			,,	,,	,,	
1869	*Glory of the Seas*	- 2009 tons (A)		,,	,,	,,	,,

NOTE.—A = American tonnage.

Reg. = Lloyd's Register net tonnage.

APPENDIX V.

Best Passages across the Atlantic.

PACKET SHIPS (Eastward).

Date.	Name	From	Time		Remarks
1848	*Richard Alsop*	Sandy Hook to Holyhead	14 days		Maiden trip
1851	*Daniel Webster*	Boston to Liverpool	13d 10h		,,
1852	*Fidelia*	Boston to N.W. Lt.ship	13	7	Capt.Furber
,, Feb.	*Washington*	New York to Liverpool	13	14	Capt. Page
,, May	*Jacob A. Westervelt*	,, ,,	14	12	—
1854 Dec.	*Dreadnought*	,, ,,	13	11	—
1859 Mar.	,,	,, ,,	13	9	—
1864	*Adelaide*	,, ,,	12	8	—

PACKET SHIPS (Westward).

Date.	Name	From	Time		Remarks
1824 Feb.	*Emerald*	Liverpool to Boston	17 days		Capt. P. Fox
185-	*Fidelia*	N.W. Ltship to Sandy Hook	17d 6h		—
,, May	*Waterloo*	Liverpool to New York	18d		—
,, Oct.	*Nabob*	London to Boston	18	6	—
,, Jan.	*Driver*	Liverpool to New York	19		—
1854 Feb.	*Dreadnought*	,, ,,	19		—

CLIPPER SHIPS (Eastward).

1853 June *Sovereign of the Seas*, New York to Liverpool, 13 days 23 hrs.
   Best 24-hour runs 344 and 340.

1853   *Typhoon*, Portsmouth N.H. to Liverpool, 13 days 12 hrs.
   In ballast. Best run 346 miles.

1854 Jan. *Red Jacket*, Sandy Hook to Rock Light, 13 days 1 hour.
   Daily runs—103, 150, 265, 232, 210, 106, 119, 300, 417,
   364, 342, 300, 360.

1854 Feb. *Lightning*, Boston Light to Rock Light, 13 days 19½ hours.
   Daily runs—200, 328, 145, 114, 110, 312, 285, 295, 260,
   306, 436.

1854 June *Champion of the Seas*, New York to Liverpool, 16 days

1854 Sept. *James Baines*, Boston Light to Rock Light, 12 days 6 hours.
   Daily runs—225, 238, 218, 305, 280, 198, 342, 200, 230,
   291, 337, 296.

1854 Oct. *Blue Jacket*, Boston Light to Cape Clear, 12 days 10 hours.

„   Nov. *White Star*, St. John to Liverpool, 15 days.   Head winds all the way.

1855 Feb. *Donald MacKay*, Boston Light to Cape Clear, 12 days.   Best run 421 miles.

1855   *Mary Whiteridge*, Baltimore to Liverpool, 13 days 7 hours.

1855   *Great Republic*, New York to Scilly, 13 days.

YACHTS (Eastward).

1851 July *America*, schooner, Sandy Hook to Havre, 21 days, in cruising rig.

1866 Dec. *Henrietta*, schooner, Sandy Hook to Isle of Wight, 13 days 22 hours.   Best run 280 miles.

„   „   *Fleetwing*, schooner, Sandy Hook to Isle of Wight, 14 days 6 hours 10 mins.   Best run 260 miles.

„   „   *Vesta*, schooner, Sandy Hook to Isle of Wight, 14 days 6 hours 50 min.   Best run 277 miles.

1868 July *Sappho*, schooner, Sandy Hook to Falmouth, 14 days (with a deep sea skipper and crew).

1869   *Sappho*, schooner, Sandy Hook to Queenstown, 12 days 9½ hours, with racing spars and racing crew.   Best run 316 miles.

1887 Mar. *Coronet*, schooner, Bay Ridge to Queenstown, 14 days 20 hours 30 mins.   Best run 291 miles.

„   „   *Dauntless*, schooner, Bay Ridge to Queenstown, 16 days 1 hour 43 mins.   Best run 326 miles.

1900   *Endymion*, schooner, Sandy Hook to Needles, 13 days 20 hours.   Best run 304 miles, lowest 250 miles.

1905 May *Endymion*, Sandy Hook to Lizard, 14 days.   Best run 291 miles.

„   „   *Atlantic* (3-mast schooner) Sandy Hook to Lizard, 12 days 4 hours.   Daily runs—165, 222, 229, 270, 113, 243, 341, 276, 243, 309.

1905 May *Valhalla* (ship), Sandy Hook to Lizard, 14 days.   Daily runs—136, 162, 225, 256, 184, 240, 287, 310, 289, 278, 280, 278, 156, 88.

1905 May *Sunbeam* (3-mast topsail schooner) Sandy Hook to Lizard—14 days 6 hours.   Daily runs—112, 198, 230, 227, 117, 243, 272, 282, 270, 250, 246, 120, 146, 125.

YACHTS (Westward).

1890 July *Cambria* (schooner), Old Hd. of Kinsale to Sandy Hook—23 days 5 hours.   Best run—220.

„   „   *Dauntless* (schooner), Old Hd. of Kinsale to Sandy Hook—23 days 7 hours.   Best run—225.

There are a number of passages claimed for certain ships which I have not included, as there is not quite sufficient proof. Of such is the *Dreadnought's* 9 days 17 hours to Queenstown. An American pilot-boat, hired by a financier for the purpose of beating the mails to Europe, which were being carried by the packet ship *Stephen Whitney*, is supposed to have crossed from Sandy Hook to Queenstown in 11 days. The famous American clipper *N. B. Palmer* has been credited with a run of 9 days to the Lizard from Sandy Hook.

But the most remarkable record claimed for an Atlantic passage is that of the wonderful four masted ship *Lancing* (*ex* the trans-Atlantic steamer *Pereire*). In February, 1916, she is said to have run from New York to Cape Wrath in 6 days 18 hours, loaded with oil cake.

INDEX.

INDEX.

A CATALOG OF SELECTED
DOVER BOOKS
IN ALL FIELDS OF INTEREST

A CATALOG OF SELECTED DOVER BOOKS IN ALL FIELDS OF INTEREST

CONCERNING THE SPIRITUAL IN ART, Wassily Kandinsky. Pioneering work by father of abstract art. Thoughts on color theory, nature of art. Analysis of earlier masters. 12 illustrations. 80pp. of text. 5⅜ × 8½. 23411-8 Pa. $2.95

LEONARDO ON THE HUMAN BODY, Leonardo da Vinci. More than 1200 of Leonardo's anatomical drawings on 215 plates. Leonardo's text, which accompanies the drawings, has been translated into English. 506pp. 8⅜ × 11¾. 24483-0 Pa. $11.95

GOBLIN MARKET, Christina Rossetti. Best-known work by poet comparable to Emily Dickinson, Alfred Tennyson. With 46 delightfully grotesque illustrations by Laurence Housman. 64pp. 4 × 6¾. 24516-0 Pa. $2.50

THE HEART OF THOREAU'S JOURNALS, edited by Odell Shepard. Selections from *Journal*, ranging over full gamut of interests. 228pp. 5⅜ × 8½. 20741-2 Pa. $4.50

MR. LINCOLN'S CAMERA MAN: MATHEW B. BRADY, Roy Meredith. Over 300 Brady photos reproduced directly from original negatives, photos. Lively commentary. 368pp. 8⅜ × 11¼. 23021-X Pa. $14.95

PHOTOGRAPHIC VIEWS OF SHERMAN'S CAMPAIGN, George N. Barnard. Reprint of landmark 1866 volume with 61 plates: battlefield of New Hope Church, the Etawah Bridge, the capture of Atlanta, etc. 80pp. 9 × 12. 23445-2 Pa. $6.00

A SHORT HISTORY OF ANATOMY AND PHYSIOLOGY FROM THE GREEKS TO HARVEY, Dr. Charles Singer. Thoroughly engrossing non-technical survey. 270 illustrations. 211pp. 5⅜ × 8½. 20389-1 Pa. $4.95

REDOUTE ROSES IRON-ON TRANSFER PATTERNS, Barbara Christopher. Redouté was botanical painter to the Empress Josephine; transfer his famous roses onto fabric with these 24 transfer patterns. 80pp. 8¼ × 10⅞. 24292-7 Pa. $3.50

THE FIVE BOOKS OF ARCHITECTURE, Sebastiano Serlio. Architectural milestone, first (1611) English translation of Renaissance classic. Unabridged reproduction of original edition includes over 300 woodcut illustrations. 416pp. 9⅜ × 12¼. 24349-4 Pa. $14.95

CARLSON'S GUIDE TO LANDSCAPE PAINTING, John F. Carlson. Authoritative, comprehensive guide covers, every aspect of landscape painting. 34 reproductions of paintings by author; 58 explanatory diagrams. 144pp. 8⅜ × 11. 22927-0 Pa. $5.95

101 PUZZLES IN THOUGHT AND LOGIC, C.R. Wylie, Jr. Solve murders, robberies, see which fishermen are liars—purely by reasoning! 107pp. 5⅜ × 8½. 20367-0 Pa. $2.00

TEST YOUR LOGIC, George J. Summers. 50 more truly new puzzles with new turns of thought, new subtleties of inference. 100pp. 5⅜ × 8½. 22877-0 Pa. $2.50

THE MURDER BOOK OF J.G. REEDER, Edgar Wallace. Eight suspenseful stories by bestselling mystery writer of 20s and 30s. Features the donnish Mr. J.G. Reeder of Public Prosecutor's Office. 128pp. 5⅜ × 8½.
24374-5 Pa. $3.95

ANNE ORR'S CHARTED DESIGNS, Anne Orr. Best designs by premier needlework designer, all on charts: flowers, borders, birds, children, alphabets, etc. Over 100 charts, 10 in color. Total of 40pp. 8¼ × 11. 23704-4 Pa. $2.50

BASIC CONSTRUCTION TECHNIQUES FOR HOUSES AND SMALL BUILDINGS SIMPLY EXPLAINED, U.S. Bureau of Naval Personnel. Grading, masonry, woodworking, floor and wall framing, roof framing, plastering, tile setting, much more. Over 675 illustrations. 568pp. 6½ × 9¼. 20242-9 Pa. $9.95

MATISSE LINE DRAWINGS AND PRINTS, Henri Matisse. Representative collection of female nudes, faces, still lifes, experimental works, etc., from 1898 to 1948. 50 illustrations. 48pp. 8⅜ × 11¼. 23877-6 Pa. $3.50

HOW TO PLAY THE CHESS OPENINGS, Eugene Znosko-Borovsky. Clear, profound examinations of just what each opening is intended to do and how opponent can counter. Many sample games. 147pp. 5⅜ × 8½. 22795-2 Pa. $3.50

DUPLICATE BRIDGE, Alfred Sheinwold. Clear, thorough, easily followed account: rules, etiquette, scoring, strategy, bidding; Goren's point-count system, Blackwood and Gerber conventions, etc. 158pp. 5⅜ × 8½. 22741-3 Pa. $3.50

SARGENT PORTRAIT DRAWINGS, J.S. Sargent. Collection of 42 portraits reveals technical skill and intuitive eye of noted American portrait painter, John Singer Sargent. 48pp. 8¼ × 11⅛. 24524-1 Pa. $3.50

ENTERTAINING SCIENCE EXPERIMENTS WITH EVERYDAY OBJECTS, Martin Gardner. Over 100 experiments for youngsters. Will amuse, astonish, teach, and entertain. Over 100 illustrations. 127pp. 5⅜ × 8½. 24201-3 Pa. $2.50

TEDDY BEAR PAPER DOLLS IN FULL COLOR: A Family of Four Bears and Their Costumes, Crystal Collins. A family of four Teddy Bear paper dolls and nearly 60 cut-out costumes. Full color, printed one side only. 32pp. 9¼ × 12¼.
24550-0 Pa. $3.50

NEW CALLIGRAPHIC ORNAMENTS AND FLOURISHES, Arthur Baker. Unusual, multi-useable material: arrows, pointing hands, brackets and frames, ovals, swirls, birds, etc. Nearly 700 illustrations. 80pp. 8⅜ × 11¼.
24095-9 Pa. $3.75

DINOSAUR DIORAMAS TO CUT & ASSEMBLE, M. Kalmenoff. Two complete three-dimensional scenes in full color, with 31 cut-out animals and plants. Excellent educational toy for youngsters. Instructions; 2 assembly diagrams. 32pp. 9¼ × 12¼. 24541-1 Pa. $4.50

SILHOUETTES: A PICTORIAL ARCHIVE OF VARIED ILLUSTRATIONS, edited by Carol Belanger Grafton. Over 600 silhouettes from the 18th to 20th centuries. Profiles and full figures of men, women, children, birds, animals, groups and scenes, nature, ships, an alphabet. 144pp. 8⅜ × 11¼. 23781-8 Pa. $5.95

25 KITES THAT FLY, Leslie Hunt. Full, easy-to-follow instructions for kites made from inexpensive materials. Many novelties. 70 illustrations. 110pp. 5⅜ × 8½.
22550-X Pa. $2.50

PIANO TUNING, J. Cree Fischer. Clearest, best book for beginner, amateur. Simple repairs, raising dropped notes, tuning by easy method of flattened fifths. No previous skills needed. 4 illustrations. 201pp. 5⅜ × 8½.   23267-0 Pa. $3.50

EARLY AMERICAN IRON-ON TRANSFER PATTERNS, edited by Rita Weiss. 75 designs, borders, alphabets, from traditional American sources. 48pp. 8¼ × 11.
23162-3 Pa. $1.95

CROCHETING EDGINGS, edited by Rita Weiss. Over 100 of the best designs for these lovely trims for a host of household items. Complete instructions, illustrations. 48pp. 8¼ × 11.   24031-2 Pa. $2.95

FINGER PLAYS FOR NURSERY AND KINDERGARTEN, Emilie Poulsson. 18 finger plays with music (voice and piano); entertaining, instructive. Counting, nature lore, etc. Victorian classic. 53 illustrations. 80pp. 6½ × 9¼. 22588-7 Pa. $2.25

BOSTON THEN AND NOW, Peter Vanderwarker. Here in 59 side-by-side views are photographic documentations of the city's past and present. 119 photographs. Full captions. 122pp. 8¼ × 11.   24312-5 Pa. $7.95

CROCHETING BEDSPREADS, edited by Rita Weiss. 22 patterns, originally published in three instruction books 1939-41. 39 photos, 8 charts. Instructions. 48pp. 8¼ × 11.   23610-2 Pa. $2.00

HAWTHORNE ON PAINTING, Charles W. Hawthorne. Collected from notes taken by students at famous Cape Cod School; hundreds of direct, personal *apercus*, ideas, suggestions. 91pp. 5⅜ × 8½.   20653-X Pa. $2.95

THERMODYNAMICS, Enrico Fermi. A classic of modern science. Clear, organized treatment of systems, first and second laws, entropy, thermodynamic potentials, etc. Calculus required. 160pp. 5⅜ × 8½.   60361-X Pa. $4.50

TEN BOOKS ON ARCHITECTURE, Vitruvius. The most important book ever written on architecture. Early Roman aesthetics, technology, classical orders, site selection, all other aspects. Morgan translation. 331pp. 5⅜ × 8½. 20645-9 Pa. $6.95

THE CORNELL BREAD BOOK, Clive M. McCay and Jeanette B. McCay. Famed high-protein recipe incorporated into breads, rolls, buns, coffee cakes, pizza, pie crusts, more. Nearly 50 illustrations. 48pp. 8¼ × 11.   23995-0 Pa. $2.00

THE CRAFTSMAN'S HANDBOOK, Cennino Cennini. 15th-century handbook, school of Giotto, explains applying gold, silver leaf; gesso; fresco painting, grinding pigments, etc. 142pp. 6⅛ × 9¼.   20054-X Pa. $3.95

FRANK LLOYD WRIGHT'S FALLINGWATER, Donald Hoffmann. Full story of Wright's masterwork at Bear Run, Pa. 100 photographs of site, construction, and details of completed structure. 112pp. 9¼ × 10.   23671-4 Pa. $7.95

OVAL STAINED GLASS PATTERN BOOK, C. Eaton. 60 new designs framed in shape of an oval. Greater complexity, challenge with sinuous cats, birds, mandalas framed in antique shape. 64pp. 8¼ × 11.   24519-5 Pa. $3.95

THE BOOK OF WOOD CARVING, Charles Marshall Sayers. Still finest book for beginning student. Fundamentals, technique; gives 34 designs, over 34 projects for panels, bookends, mirrors, etc. 33 photos. 118pp. 7¾ × 10⅝. 23654-4 Pa. $3.95

CARVING COUNTRY CHARACTERS, Bill Higginbotham. Expert advice for beginning, advanced carvers on materials, techniques for creating 18 projects—mirthful panorama of American characters. 105 illustrations. 80pp. 8⅜ × 11. 24135-1 Pa. $2.95

300 ART NOUVEAU DESIGNS AND MOTIFS IN FULL COLOR, C.B. Grafton. 44 full-page plates display swirling lines and muted colors typical of Art Nouveau. Borders, frames, panels, cartouches, dingbats, etc. 48pp. 9⅜ × 12¼. 24354-0 Pa. $6.95

SELF-WORKING CARD TRICKS, Karl Fulves. Editor of *Pallbearer* offers 72 tricks that work automatically through nature of card deck. No sleight of hand needed. Often spectacular. 42 illustrations. 113pp. 5⅜ × 8½. 23334-0 Pa. $3.50

CUT AND ASSEMBLE A WESTERN FRONTIER TOWN, Edmund V. Gillon, Jr. Ten authentic full-color buildings on heavy cardboard stock in H-O scale. Sheriff's Office and Jail, Saloon, Wells Fargo, Opera House, others. 48pp. 9¼ × 12¼. 23736-2 Pa. $4.95

CUT AND ASSEMBLE AN EARLY NEW ENGLAND VILLAGE, Edmund V. Gillon, Jr. Printed in full color on heavy cardboard stock. 12 authentic buildings in H-O scale: Adams home in Quincy, Mass., Oliver Wight house in Sturbridge, smithy, store, church, others. 48pp. 9¼ × 12¼. 23536-X Pa. $4.95

THE TALE OF TWO BAD MICE, Beatrix Potter. Tom Thumb and Hunca Munca squeeze out of their hole and go exploring. 27 full-color Potter illustrations. 59pp. 4¼ × 5½. (Available in U.S. only) 23065-1 Pa. $1.75

CARVING FIGURE CARICATURES IN THE OZARK STYLE, Harold L. Enlow. Instructions and illustrations for ten delightful projects, plus general carving instructions. 22 drawings and 47 photographs altogether. 39pp. 8⅜ × 11. 23151-8 Pa. $2.95

A TREASURY OF FLOWER DESIGNS FOR ARTISTS, EMBROIDERERS AND CRAFTSMEN, Susan Gaber. 100 garden favorites lushly rendered by artist for artists, craftsmen, needleworkers. Many form frames, borders. 80pp. 8¼ × 11. 24096-7 Pa. $3.95

CUT & ASSEMBLE A TOY THEATER/THE NUTCRACKER BALLET, Tom Tierney. Model of a complete, full-color production of Tchaikovsky's classic. 6 backdrops, dozens of characters, familiar dance sequences. 32pp. 9⅜ × 12¼. 24194-7 Pa. $4.50

ANIMALS: 1,419 COPYRIGHT-FREE ILLUSTRATIONS OF MAMMALS, BIRDS, FISH, INSECTS, ETC., edited by Jim Harter. Clear wood engravings present, in extremely lifelike poses, over 1,000 species of animals. 284pp. 9 × 12. 23766-4 Pa. $9.95

MORE HAND SHADOWS, Henry Bursill. For those at their 'finger ends," 16 more effects—Shakespeare, a hare, a squirrel, Mr. Punch, and twelve more—each explained by a full-page illustration. Considerable period charm. 30pp. 6½ × 9¼. 21384-6 Pa. $1.95

SURREAL STICKERS AND UNREAL STAMPS, William Rowe. 224 haunting, hilarious stamps on gummed, perforated stock, with images of elephants, geisha girls, George Washington, etc. 16pp. one side. 8¼ × 11. 24371-0 Pa. $3.50

GOURMET KITCHEN LABELS, Ed Sibbett, Jr. 112 full-color labels (4 copies each of 28 designs). Fruit, bread, other culinary motifs. Gummed and perforated. 16pp. 8¼ × 11. 24087-8 Pa. $2.95

PATTERNS AND INSTRUCTIONS FOR CARVING AUTHENTIC BIRDS, H.D. Green. Detailed instructions, 27 diagrams, 85 photographs for carving 15 species of birds so life-like, they'll seem ready to fly! 8¼ × 11. 24222-6 Pa. $3.00

FLATLAND, E.A. Abbott. Science-fiction classic explores life of 2-D being in 3-D world. 16 illustrations. 103pp. 5⅜ × 8. 20001-9 Pa. $2.00

DRIED FLOWERS, Sarah Whitlock and Martha Rankin. Concise, clear, practical guide to dehydration, glycerinizing, pressing plant material, and more. Covers use of silica gel. 12 drawings. 32pp. 5⅜ × 8½. 21802-3 Pa. $1.00

EASY-TO-MAKE CANDLES, Gary V. Guy. Learn how easy it is to make all kinds of decorative candles. Step-by-step instructions. 82 illustrations. 48pp. 8¼ × 11.
23881-4 Pa. $2.95

SUPER STICKERS FOR KIDS, Carolyn Bracken. 128 gummed and perforated full-color stickers: GIRL WANTED, KEEP OUT, BORED OF EDUCATION, X-RATED, COMBAT ZONE, many others. 16pp. 8¼ × 11. 24092-4 Pa. $3.50

CUT AND COLOR PAPER MASKS, Michael Grater. Clowns, animals, funny faces...simply color them in, cut them out, and put them together, and you have 9 paper masks to play with and enjoy. 32pp. 8¼ × 11. 23171-2 Pa. $2.95

A CHRISTMAS CAROL: THE ORIGINAL MANUSCRIPT, Charles Dickens. Clear facsimile of Dickens manuscript, on facing pages with final printed text. 8 illustrations by John Leech, 4 in color on covers. 144pp. 8⅜ × 11¼.
20980-6 Pa. $5.95

CARVING SHOREBIRDS, Harry V. Shourds & Anthony Hillman. 16 full-size patterns (all double-page spreads) for 19 North American shorebirds with step-by-step instructions. 72pp. 9¼ × 12¼. 24287-0 Pa. $5.95

THE GENTLE ART OF MATHEMATICS, Dan Pedoe. Mathematical games, probability, the question of infinity, topology, how the laws of algebra work, problems of irrational numbers, and more. 42 figures. 143pp. 5⅜ × 8½.
22949-1 Pa. $3.50

READY-TO-USE DOLLHOUSE WALLPAPER, Katzenbach & Warren, Inc. Stripe, 2 floral stripes, 2 allover florals, polka dot; all in full color. 4 sheets (350 sq. in.) of each, enough for average room. 48pp. 8¼ × 11. 23495-9 Pa. $2.95

MINIATURE IRON-ON TRANSFER PATTERNS FOR DOLLHOUSES, DOLLS, AND SMALL PROJECTS, Rita Weiss and Frank Fontana. Over 100 miniature patterns: rugs, bedspreads, quilts, chair seats, etc. In standard dollhouse size. 48pp. 8¼ × 11. 23741-9 Pa. $1.95

THE DINOSAUR COLORING BOOK, Anthony Rao. 45 renderings of dinosaurs, fossil birds, turtles, other creatures of Mesozoic Era. Scientifically accurate. Captions. 48pp. 8¼ × 11. 24022-3 Pa. $2.50

JAPANESE DESIGN MOTIFS, Matsuya Co. Mon, or heraldic designs. Over 4000 typical, beautiful designs: birds, animals, flowers, swords, fans, geometrics; all beautifully stylized. 213pp. 11⅜ × 8¼. 22874-6 Pa. $7.95

THE TALE OF BENJAMIN BUNNY, Beatrix Potter. Peter Rabbit's cousin coaxes him back into Mr. McGregor's garden for a whole new set of adventures. All 27 full-color illustrations. 59pp. 4¼ × 5½. (Available in U.S. only) 21102-9 Pa. $1.75

THE TALE OF PETER RABBIT AND OTHER FAVORITE STORIES BOXED SET, Beatrix Potter. Seven of Beatrix Potter's best-loved tales including Peter Rabbit in a specially designed, durable boxed set. 4¼ × 5½. Total of 447pp. 158 color illustrations. (Available in U.S. only) 23903-9 Pa. $12.25

PRACTICAL MENTAL MAGIC, Theodore Annemann. Nearly 200 astonishing feats of mental magic revealed in step-by-step detail. Complete advice on staging, patter, etc. Illustrated. 320pp. 5⅜ × 8½. 24426-1 Pa. $5.95

CELEBRATED CASES OF JUDGE DEE (DEE GOONG AN), translated by Robert Van Gulik. Authentic 18th-century Chinese detective novel; Dee and associates solve three interlocked cases. Led to van Gulik's own stories with same characters. Extensive introduction. 9 illustrations. 237pp. 5⅜ × 8½. 23337-5 Pa. $4.95

CUT & FOLD EXTRATERRESTRIAL INVADERS THAT FLY, M. Grater. Stage your own lilliputian space battles.By following the step-by-step instructions and explanatory diagrams you can launch 22 full-color fliers into space. 36pp. 8¼ × 11. 24478-4 Pa. $2.95

CUT & ASSEMBLE VICTORIAN HOUSES, Edmund V. Gillon, Jr. Printed in full color on heavy cardboard stock, 4 authentic Victorian houses in H-O scale: Italian-style Villa, Octagon, Second Empire, Stick Style. 48pp. 9¼ × 12¼. 23849-0 Pa. $4.95

BEST SCIENCE FICTION STORIES OF H.G. WELLS, H.G. Wells. Full novel *The Invisible Man,* plus 17 short stories: "The Crystal Egg," "Aepyornis Island," "The Strange Orchid," etc. 303pp. 5⅜ × 8½. (Available in U.S. only) 21531-8 Pa. $4.95

TRADEMARK DESIGNS OF THE WORLD, Yusaku Kamekura. A lavish collection of nearly 700 trademarks, the work of Wright, Loewy, Klee, Binder, hundreds of others. 160pp. 8¾ × 8. (EJ) 24191-2 Pa. $5.95

THE ARTIST'S AND CRAFTSMAN'S GUIDE TO REDUCING, ENLARGING AND TRANSFERRING DESIGNS, Rita Weiss. Discover, reduce, enlarge, transfer designs from any objects to any craft project. 12pp. plus 16 sheets special graph paper. 8¼ × 11. 24142-4 Pa. $3.95

TREASURY OF JAPANESE DESIGNS AND MOTIFS FOR ARTISTS AND CRAFTSMEN, edited by Carol Belanger Grafton. Indispensable collection of 360 traditional Japanese designs and motifs redrawn in clean, crisp black-and-white, copyright-free illustrations. 96pp. 8¼ × 11. 24435-0 Pa. $4.50

CHANCERY CURSIVE STROKE BY STROKE, Arthur Baker. Instructions and illustrations for each stroke of each letter (upper and lower case) and numerals. 54 full-page plates. 64pp. 8¼ × 11.   24278-1 Pa. $2.50

THE ENJOYMENT AND USE OF COLOR, Walter Sargent. Color relationships, values, intensities; complementary colors, illumination, similar topics. Color in nature and art. 7 color plates, 29 illustrations. 274pp. 5⅜ × 8½.   20944-X Pa. $4.95

SCULPTURE PRINCIPLES AND PRACTICE, Louis Slobodkin. Step-by-step approach to clay, plaster, metals, stone; classical and modern. 253 drawings, photos. 255pp. 8⅛ × 11.   22960-2 Pa. $7.50

VICTORIAN FASHION PAPER DOLLS FROM HARPER'S BAZAR, 1867-1898, Theodore Menten. Four female dolls with 28 elegant high fashion costumes, printed in full color. 32pp. 9¼ × 12¼.   23453-3 Pa. $3.95

FLOPSY, MOPSY AND COTTONTAIL: A Little Book of Paper Dolls in Full Color, Susan LaBelle. Three dolls and 21 costumes (7 for each doll) show Peter Rabbit's siblings dressed for holidays, gardening, hiking, etc. Charming borders, captions. 48pp. 4¼ × 5½. (USCO)   24376-1 Pa. $2.50

NATIONAL LEAGUE BASEBALL CARD CLASSICS, Bert Randolph Sugar. 83 big-leaguers from 1909-69 on facsimile cards. Hubbell, Dean, Spahn, Brock plus advertising, info, no duplications. Perforated, detachable. 16pp. 8¼ × 11.
                                                                24308-7 Pa. $3.50

THE LOGICAL APPROACH TO CHESS, Dr. Max Euwe, et al. First-rate text of comprehensive strategy, tactics, theory for the amateur. No gambits to memorize, just a clear, logical approach. 224pp. 5⅜ × 8½.   24353-2 Pa. $4.50

MAGICK IN THEORY AND PRACTICE, Aleister Crowley. The summation of the thought and practice of the century's most famous necromancer, long hard to find. Crowley's best book. 436pp. 5⅜ × 8½. (Available in U.S. only)
                                                                23295-6 Pa. $6.95

THE HAUNTED HOTEL, Wilkie Collins. Collins' last great tale; doom and destiny in a Venetian palace. Praised by T.S. Eliot. 127pp. 5⅜ × 8½.
                                                                24333-8 Pa. $3.00

ART DECO DISPLAY ALPHABETS, Dan X. Solo. Wide variety of bold yet elegant lettering in handsome Art Deco styles. 100 complete fonts, with numerals, punctuation, more. 104pp. 8⅛ × 11.   24372-9 Pa. $4.50

CALLIGRAPHIC ALPHABETS, Arthur Baker. Nearly 150 complete alphabets by outstanding contemporary. Stimulating ideas; useful source for unique effects. 154 plates. 157pp. 8⅜ × 11¼.   21045-6 Pa. $5.95

ARTHUR BAKER'S HISTORIC CALLIGRAPHIC ALPHABETS, Arthur Baker. From monumental capitals of first-century Rome to humanistic cursive of 16th century, 33 alphabets in fresh interpretations. 88 plates. 96pp. 9 × 12.
                                                                24054-1 Pa. $4.50

LETTIE LANE PAPER DOLLS, Sheila Young. Genteel turn-of-the-century family very popular then and now. 24 paper dolls. 16 plates in full color. 32pp. 9¼ × 12¼.   24089-4 Pa. $3.95

KEYBOARD WORKS FOR SOLO INSTRUMENTS, G.F. Handel. 35 neglected works from Handel's vast oeuvre, originally jotted down as improvisations. Includes Eight Great Suites, others. New sequence. 174pp. 9⅜ × 12¼.
24338-9 Pa. $7.50

AMERICAN LEAGUE BASEBALL CARD CLASSICS, Bert Randolph Sugar. 82 stars from 1900s to 60s on facsimile cards. Ruth, Cobb, Mantle, Williams, plus advertising, info, no duplications. Perforated, detachable. 16pp. 8¼ × 11.
24286-2 Pa. $3.50

A TREASURY OF CHARTED DESIGNS FOR NEEDLEWORKERS, Georgia Gorham and Jeanne Warth. 141 charted designs: owl, cat with yarn, tulips, piano, spinning wheel, covered bridge, Victorian house and many others. 48pp. 8¼ × 11.
23558-0 Pa. $1.95

DANISH FLORAL CHARTED DESIGNS, Gerda Bengtsson. Exquisite collection of over 40 different florals: anemone, Iceland poppy, wild fruit, pansies, many others. 45 illustrations. 48pp. 8¼ × 11.
23957-8 Pa. $2.50

OLD PHILADELPHIA IN EARLY PHOTOGRAPHS 1839-1914, Robert F. Looney. 215 photographs: panoramas, street scenes, landmarks, President-elect Lincoln's visit, 1876 Centennial Exposition, much more. 230pp. 8⅜ × 11¾.
23345-6 Pa. $9.95

PRELUDE TO MATHEMATICS, W.W. Sawyer. Noted mathematician's lively, stimulating account of non-Euclidean geometry, matrices, determinants, group theory, other topics. Emphasis on novel, striking aspects. 224pp. 5⅜ × 8½.
24401-6 Pa. $4.50

ADVENTURES WITH A MICROSCOPE, Richard Headstrom. 59 adventures with clothing fibers, protozoa, ferns and lichens, roots and leaves, much more. 142 illustrations. 232pp. 5⅜ × 8½.
23471-1 Pa. $3.95

IDENTIFYING ANIMAL TRACKS: MAMMALS, BIRDS, AND OTHER ANIMALS OF THE EASTERN UNITED STATES, Richard Headstrom. For hunters, naturalists, scouts, nature-lovers. Diagrams of tracks, tips on identification. 128pp. 5⅜ × 8.
24442-3 Pa. $3.50

VICTORIAN FASHIONS AND COSTUMES FROM HARPER'S BAZAR, 1867-1898, edited by Stella Blum. Day costumes, evening wear, sports clothes, shoes, hats, other accessories in over 1,000 detailed engravings. 320pp. 9⅜ × 12¼.
22990-4 Pa. $10.95

EVERYDAY FASHIONS OF THE TWENTIES AS PICTURED IN SEARS AND OTHER CATALOGS, edited by Stella Blum. Actual dress of the Roaring Twenties, with text by Stella Blum. Over 750 illustrations, captions. 156pp. 9 × 12.
24134-3 Pa. $8.95

HALL OF FAME BASEBALL CARDS, edited by Bert Randolph Sugar. Cy Young, Ted Williams, Lou Gehrig, and many other Hall of Fame greats on 92 full-color, detachable reprints of early baseball cards. No duplication of cards with *Classic Baseball Cards.* 16pp. 8¼ × 11.
23624-2 Pa. $3.50

THE ART OF HAND LETTERING, Helm Wotzkow. Course in hand lettering, Roman, Gothic, Italic, Block, Script. Tools, proportions, optical aspects, individual variation. Very quality conscious. Hundreds of specimens. 320pp. 5⅜ × 8½.
21797-3 Pa. $5.95

HOW THE OTHER HALF LIVES, Jacob A. Riis. Journalistic record of filth, degradation, upward drive in New York immigrant slums, shops, around 1900. New edition includes 100 original Riis photos, monuments of early photography. 233pp. 10 × 7⅞.   22012-5 Pa. $9.95

CHINA AND ITS PEOPLE IN EARLY PHOTOGRAPHS, John Thomson. In 200 black-and-white photographs of exceptional quality photographic pioneer Thomson captures the mountains, dwellings, monuments and people of 19th-century China. 272pp. 9⅜ × 12¼.   24393-1 Pa. $13.95

GODEY COSTUME PLATES IN COLOR FOR DECOUPAGE AND FRAM-ING, edited by Eleanor Hasbrouk Rawlings. 24 full-color engravings depicting 19th-century Parisian haute couture. Printed on one side only. 56pp. 8¼ × 11.   23879-2 Pa. $3.95

ART NOUVEAU STAINED GLASS PATTERN BOOK, Ed Sibbett, Jr. 104 projects using well-known themes of Art Nouveau: swirling forms, florals, peacocks, and sensuous women. 60pp. 8¼ × 11.   23577-7 Pa. $3.95

QUICK AND EASY PATCHWORK ON THE SEWING MACHINE: Susan Aylsworth Murwin and Suzzy Payne. Instructions, diagrams show exactly how to machine sew 12 quilts. 48pp. of templates. 50 figures. 80pp. 8¼ × 11.
                                                                                    23770-2 Pa. $3.95

THE STANDARD BOOK OF QUILT MAKING AND COLLECTING, Marguerite Ickis. Full information, full-sized patterns for making 46 traditional quilts, also 150 other patterns. 483 illustrations. 273pp. 6⅞ × 9⅝. 20582-7 Pa. $5.95

LETTERING AND ALPHABETS, J. Albert Cavanagh. 85 complete alphabets lettered in various styles; instructions for spacing, roughs, brushwork. 121pp. 8¾ × 8.   20053-1 Pa. $3.95

LETTER FORMS: 110 COMPLETE ALPHABETS, Frederick Lambert. 110 sets of capital letters; 16 lower case alphabets; 70 sets of numbers and other symbols. 110pp. 8⅛ × 11.   22872-X Pa. $4.50

ORCHIDS AS HOUSE PLANTS, Rebecca Tyson Northen. Grow cattleyas and many other kinds of orchids—in a window, in a case, or under artificial light. 63 illustrations. 148pp. 5⅜ × 8½.   23261-1 Pa. $2.95

THE MUSHROOM HANDBOOK, Louis C.C. Krieger. Still the best popular handbook. Full descriptions of 259 species, extremely thorough text, poisons, folklore, etc. 32 color plates; 126 other illustrations. 560pp. 5⅜ × 8½.
                                                                                    21861-9 Pa. $8.50

THE DORÉ BIBLE ILLUSTRATIONS, Gustave Doré. All wonderful, detailed plates: Adam and Eve, Flood, Babylon, life of Jesus, etc. Brief King James text with each plate. 241 plates. 241pp. 9 × 12.   23004-X Pa. $8.95

THE BOOK OF KELLS: Selected Plates in Full Color, edited by Blanche Cirker. 32 full-page plates from greatest manuscript-icon of early Middle Ages. Fantastic, mysterious. Publisher's Note. Captions. 32pp. 9¾ × 12¼.   24345-1 Pa. $4.50

THE PERFECT WAGNERITE, George Bernard Shaw. Brilliant criticism of the Ring Cycle, with provocative interpretation of politics, economic theories behind the Ring. 136pp. 5⅜ × 8½. (EUK)   21707-8 Pa. $3.95

THE RIME OF THE ANCIENT MARINER, Gustave Doré, S.T. Coleridge. Doré's finest work, 34 plates capture moods, subtleties of poem. Full text. 77pp. 9¼ × 12. 22305-1 Pa. $4.95

SONGS OF INNOCENCE, William Blake. The first and most popular of Blake's famous "Illuminated Books," in a facsimile edition reproducing all 31 brightly colored plates. Additional printed text of each poem. 64pp. 5¼ × 7.
22764-2 Pa. $3.50

AN INTRODUCTION TO INFORMATION THEORY, J.R. Pierce. Second (1980) edition of most impressive non-technical account available. Encoding, entropy, noisy channel, related areas, etc. 320pp. 5⅜ × 8½. 24061-4 Pa. $5.95

THE DIVINE PROPORTION: A STUDY IN MATHEMATICAL BEAUTY, H.E. Huntley. "Divine proportion" or "golden ratio" in poetry, Pascal's triangle, philosophy, psychology, music, mathematical figures, etc. Excellent bridge between science and art. 58 figures. 185pp. 5⅜ × 8½. 22254-3 Pa. $4.50

THE DOVER NEW YORK WALKING GUIDE: From the Battery to Wall Street, Mary J. Shapiro. Superb inexpensive guide to historic buildings and locales in lower Manhattan: Trinity Church, Bowling Green, more. Complete Text; maps. 36 illustrations. 48pp. 3⅞ × 9¼. 24225-0 Pa. $2.50

NEW YORK THEN AND NOW, Edward B. Watson, Edmund V. Gillon, Jr. 83 important Manhattan sites: on facing pages early photographs (1875-1925) and 1976 photos by Gillon. 172 illustrations. 171pp. 9¼ × 10. 23361-8 Pa. $9.95

HISTORIC COSTUME IN PICTURES, Braun & Schneider. Over 1450 costumed figures from dawn of civilization to end of 19th century. English captions. 125 plates. 256pp. 8⅜ × 11¼. 23150-X Pa. $7.95

VICTORIAN AND EDWARDIAN FASHION: A Photographic Survey, Alison Gernsheim. First fashion history completely illustrated by contemporary photographs. Full text plus 235 photos, 1840-1914, in which many celebrities appear. 240pp. 6½ × 9¼. 24205-6 Pa. $6.00

CHARTED CHRISTMAS DESIGNS FOR COUNTED CROSS-STITCH AND OTHER NEEDLECRAFTS, Lindberg Press. Charted designs for 45 beautiful needlecraft projects with many yuletide and wintertime motifs. 48pp. 8¼ × 11. (EDNS) 24356-7 Pa. $2.50

101 FOLK DESIGNS FOR COUNTED CROSS-STITCH AND OTHER NEEDLE-CRAFTS, Carter Houck. 101 authentic charted folk designs in a wide array of lovely representations with many suggestions for effective use. 48pp. 8¼ × 11.
24369-9 Pa. $2.25

FIVE ACRES AND INDEPENDENCE, Maurice G. Kains. Great back-to-the-land classic explains basics of self-sufficient farming. The one book to get. 95 illustrations. 397pp. 5⅜ × 8½. 20974-1 Pa. $6.50

A MODERN HERBAL, Margaret Grieve. Much the fullest, most exact, most useful compilation of herbal material. Gigantic alphabetical encyclopedia, from aconite to zedoary, gives botanical information, medical properties, folklore, economic uses, and much else. Indispensable to serious reader. 161 illustrations. 888pp. 6½ × 9¼. (Available in U.S. only) 22798-7, 22799-5 Pa., Two-vol. set $17.00

DECORATIVE NAPKIN FOLDING FOR BEGINNERS, Lillian Oppenheimer and Natalie Epstein. 22 different napkin folds in the shape of a heart, clown's hat, love knot, etc. 63 drawings. 48pp. 8¼ × 11. 23797-4 Pa. $2.25

DECORATIVE LABELS FOR HOME CANNING, PRESERVING, AND OTHER HOUSEHOLD AND GIFT USES, Theodore Menten. 128 gummed, perforated labels, beautifully printed in 2 colors. 12 versions. Adhere to metal, glass, wood, ceramics. 24pp. 8¼ × 11. 23219-0 Pa. $3.50

EARLY AMERICAN STENCILS ON WALLS AND FURNITURE, Janet Waring. Thorough coverage of 19th-century folk art: techniques, artifacts, surviving specimens. 166 illustrations, 7 in color. 147pp. of text. 7⅞ × 10¾. 21906-2 Pa. $9.95

AMERICAN ANTIQUE WEATHERVANES, A.B. & W.T. Westervelt. Extensively illustrated 1883 catalog exhibiting over 550 copper weathervanes and finials. Excellent primary source by one of the principal manufacturers. 104pp. 6⅛ × 9¼. 24396-6 Pa. $3.95

ART STUDENTS' ANATOMY, Edmond J. Farris. Long favorite in art schools. Basic elements, common positions, actions. Full text, 158 illustrations. 159pp. 5⅜ × 8½. 20744-7 Pa. $3.95

BRIDGMAN'S LIFE DRAWING, George B. Bridgman. More than 500 drawings and text teach you to abstract the body into its major masses. Also specific areas of anatomy. 192pp. 6½ × 9¼. 22710-3 Pa. $4.50

COMPLETE PRELUDES AND ETUDES FOR SOLO PIANO, Frederic Chopin. All 26 Preludes, all 27 Etudes by greatest composer of piano music. Authoritative Paderewski edition. 224pp. 9 × 12. (Available in U.S. only) 24052-5 Pa. $7.50

PIANO MUSIC 1888-1905, Claude Debussy. Deux Arabesques, Suite Bergamesque, Masques, 1st series of Images, etc. 9 others, in corrected editions. 175pp. 9⅜ × 12¼. 22771-5 Pa. $6.95

TEDDY BEAR IRON-ON TRANSFER PATTERNS, Ted Menten. 80 iron-on transfer patterns of male and female Teddys in a wide variety of activities, poses, sizes. 48pp. 8¼ × 11. 24596-9 Pa. $2.25

A PICTURE HISTORY OF THE BROOKLYN BRIDGE, M.J. Shapiro. Profusely illustrated account of greatest engineering achievement of 19th century. 167 rare photos & engravings recall construction, human drama. Extensive, detailed text. 122pp. 8¼ × 11. 24403-2 Pa. $7.95

NEW YORK IN THE THIRTIES, Berenice Abbott. Noted photographer's fascinating study shows new buildings that have become famous and old sights that have disappeared forever. 97 photographs. 97pp. 11⅜ × 10. 22967-X Pa. $7.50

MATHEMATICAL TABLES AND FORMULAS, Robert D. Carmichael and Edwin R. Smith. Logarithms, sines, tangents, trig functions, powers, roots, reciprocals, exponential and hyperbolic functions, formulas and theorems. 269pp. 5⅜ × 8½. 60111-0 Pa. $4.95

HANDBOOK OF MATHEMATICAL FUNCTIONS WITH FORMULAS, GRAPHS, AND MATHEMATICAL TABLES, edited by Milton Abramowitz and Irene A. Stegun. Vast compendium: 29 sets of tables, some to as high as 20 places. 1,046pp. 8 × 10½. 61272-4 Pa. $21.95

REASON IN ART, George Santayana. Renowned philosopher's provocative, seminal treatment of basis of art in instinct and experience. Volume Four of *The Life of Reason*. 230pp. 5⅜ × 8. 24358-3 Pa. $4.50

LANGUAGE, TRUTH AND LOGIC, Alfred J. Ayer. Famous, clear introduction to Vienna, Cambridge schools of Logical Positivism. Role of philosophy, elimination of metaphysics, nature of analysis, etc. 160pp. 5⅜ × 8½. (USCO) 20010-8 Pa. $2.95

BASIC ELECTRONICS, U.S. Bureau of Naval Personnel. Electron tubes, circuits, antennas, AM, FM, and CW transmission and receiving, etc. 560 illustrations. 567pp. 6½ × 9¼. 21076-6 Pa. $9.95

THE ART DECO STYLE, edited by Theodore Menten. Furniture, jewelry, metalwork, ceramics, fabrics, lighting fixtures, interior decors, exteriors, graphics from pure French sources. Over 400 photographs. 183pp. 8⅜ × 11¼. 22824-X Pa. $7.95

THE FOUR BOOKS OF ARCHITECTURE, Andrea Palladio. 16th-century classic covers classical architectural remains, Renaissance revivals, classical orders, etc. 1738 Ware English edition. 216 plates. 110pp. of text. 9½ × 12¾. 21308-0 Pa. $11.95

THE WIT AND HUMOR OF OSCAR WILDE, edited by Alvin Redman. More than 1000 ripostes, paradoxes, wisecracks: Work is the curse of the drinking classes, I can resist everything except temptations, etc. 258pp. 5⅜ × 8½. 20602-5 Pa. $4.50

THE DEVIL'S DICTIONARY, Ambrose Bierce. Barbed, bitter, brilliant witticisms in the form of a dictionary. Best, most ferocious satire America has produced. 145pp. 5⅜ × 8½. 20487-1 Pa. $2.95

ERTÉ'S FASHION DESIGNS, Erté. 210 black-and-white inventions from *Harper's Bazar*, 1918-32, plus 8pp. full-color covers. Captions. 88pp. 9 × 12. 24203-X Pa. $7.95

ERTÉ GRAPHICS, Erté. Collection of striking color graphics: *Seasons, Alphabet, Numerals, Aces* and *Precious Stones*. 50 plates, including 4 on covers. 48pp. 9⅜ × 12¼. 23580-7 Pa. $6.95

PAPER FOLDING FOR BEGINNERS, William D. Murray and Francis J. Rigney. Clearest book for making origami sail boats, roosters, frogs that move legs, etc. 40 projects. More than 275 illustrations. 94pp. 5⅜ × 8½. 20713-7 Pa. $2.50

ORIGAMI FOR THE ENTHUSIAST, John Montroll. Fish, ostrich, peacock, squirrel, rhinoceros, Pegasus, 19 other intricate subjects. Instructions. Diagrams. 128pp. 9 × 12. 23799-0 Pa. $5.95

CROCHETING NOVELTY POT HOLDERS, edited by Linda Macho. 64 useful, whimsical pot holders feature kitchen themes, animals, flowers, other novelties. Surprisingly easy to crochet. Complete instructions. 48pp. 8¼ × 11. 24296-X Pa. $1.95

CROCHETING DOILIES, edited by Rita Weiss. Irish Crochet, Jewel, Star Wheel, Vanity Fair and more. Also luncheon and console sets, runners and centerpieces. 51 illustrations. 48pp. 8¼ × 11. 23424-X Pa. $2.75

YUCATAN BEFORE AND AFTER THE CONQUEST, Diego de Landa. Only significant account of Yucatan written in the early post-Conquest era. Translated by William Gates. Over 120 illustrations. 162pp. 5⅜ × 8½.   23622-6 Pa. $3.95

ORNATE PICTORIAL CALLIGRAPHY, E.A. Lupfer. Complete instructions, over 150 examples help you create magnificent "flourishes" from which beautiful animals and objects gracefully emerge. 8⅛ × 11.   21957-7 Pa. $3.50

DOLLY DINGLE PAPER DOLLS, Grace Drayton. Cute chubby children by same artist who did Campbell Kids. Rare plates from 1910s. 30 paper dolls and over 100 outfits reproduced in full color. 32pp. 9¼ × 12¼.   23711-7 Pa. $3.50

CURIOUS GEORGE PAPER DOLLS IN FULL COLOR, H. A. Rey, Kathy Allert. Naughty little monkey-hero of children's books in two doll figures, plus 48 full-color costumes: pirate, Indian chief, fireman, more. 32pp. 9¼ × 12¼.
      24386-9 Pa. $3.50

GERMAN: HOW TO SPEAK AND WRITE IT, Joseph Rosenberg. Like *French, How to Speak and Write It.* Very rich modern course, with a wealth of pictorial material. 330 illustrations. 384pp. 5⅜ × 8½.   20271-2 Pa. $4.95

CATS AND KITTENS: 24 Ready-to-Mail Color Photo Postcards, D. Holby. Handsome collection; feline in a variety of adorable poses. Identifications. 12pp. on postcard stock. 8¼ × 11.   24469-5 Pa. $2.95

MARILYN MONROE PAPER DOLLS, Tom Tierney. 31 full-color designs on heavy stock, from *The Asphalt Jungle, Gentlemen Prefer Blondes,* 22 others. 1 doll. 16 plates. 32pp. 9⅜ × 12¼.   23769-9 Pa. $3.95

FUNDAMENTALS OF LAYOUT, F.H. Wills. All phases of layout design discussed and illustrated in 121 illustrations. Indispensable as student's text or handbook for professional. 124pp. 8⅛ × 11.   21279-3 Pa. $4.50

FANTASTIC SUPER STICKERS, Ed Sibbett, Jr. 75 colorful pressure-sensitive stickers. Peel off and place for a touch of pizzazz: clowns, penguins, teddy bears, etc. Full color. 16pp. 8¼ × 11.   24471-7 Pa. $3.50

LABELS FOR ALL OCCASIONS, Ed Sibbett, Jr. 6 labels each of 16 different designs—baroque, art nouveau, art deco, Pennsylvania Dutch, etc.—in full color. 24pp. 8¼ × 11.   23688-9 Pa. $3.95

HOW TO CALCULATE QUICKLY: RAPID METHODS IN BASIC MATHE-MATICS, Henry Sticker. Addition, subtraction, multiplication, division, checks, etc. More than 8000 problems, solutions. 185pp. 5 × 7¼.   20295-X Pa. $2.95

THE CAT COLORING BOOK, Karen Baldauski. Handsome, realistic renderings of 40 splendid felines, from American shorthair to exotic types. 44 plates. Captions. 48pp. 8¼ × 11.   24011-8 Pa. $2.50

THE TALE OF PETER RABBIT, Beatrix Potter. The inimitable Peter's terrifying adventure in Mr. McGregor's garden, with all 27 wonderful, full-color Potter illustrations. 55pp. 4¼ × 5½. (Available in U.S. only)   22827-4 Pa. $1.75

BASIC ELECTRICITY, U.S. Bureau of Naval Personnel. Batteries, circuits, conductors, AC and DC, inductance and capacitance, generators, motors, trans-formers, amplifiers, etc. 349 illustrations. 448pp. 6½ × 9¼.   20973-3 Pa. $7.95

SOURCE BOOK OF MEDICAL HISTORY, edited by Logan Clendening, M.D. Original accounts ranging from Ancient Egypt and Greece to discovery of X-rays: Galen, Pasteur, Lavoisier, Harvey, Parkinson, others. 685pp. 5⅜ × 8½.

20621-1 Pa. $11.95

THE ROSE AND THE KEY, J.S. Lefanu. Superb mystery novel from Irish master. Dark doings among an ancient and aristocratic English family. Well-drawn characters; capital suspense. Introduction by N. Donaldson. 448pp. 5⅜ × 8½.

24377-X Pa. $6.95

SOUTH WIND, Norman Douglas. Witty, elegant novel of ideas set on languorous Meditterranean island of Nepenthe. Elegant prose, glittering epigrams, mordant satire. 1917 masterpiece. 416pp. 5⅜ × 8½. (Available in U.S. only)

24361-3 Pa. $5.95

RUSSELL'S CIVIL WAR PHOTOGRAPHS, Capt. A.J. Russell. 116 rare Civil War Photos: Bull Run, Virginia campaigns, bridges, railroads, Richmond, Lincoln's funeral car. Many never seen before. Captions. 128pp. 9⅜ × 12¼.

24283-8 Pa. $7.95

PHOTOGRAPHS BY MAN RAY: 105 Works, 1920-1934. Nudes, still lifes, landscapes, women's faces, celebrity portraits (Dali, Matisse, Picasso, others), rayographs. Reprinted from rare gravure edition. 128pp. 9⅜ × 12¼.

23842-3 Pa. $8.95

STAR NAMES: THEIR LORE AND MEANING, Richard H. Allen. Star names, the zodiac, constellations: folklore and literature associated with heavens. The basic book of its field, fascinating reading. 563pp. 5⅜ × 8½.   21079-0 Pa. $7.95

BURNHAM'S CELESTIAL HANDBOOK, Robert Burnham, Jr. Thorough guide to the stars beyond our solar system. Exhaustive treatment. Alphabetical by constellation: Andromeda to Cetus in Vol. 1; Chamaeleon to Orion in Vol. 2; and Pavo to Vulpecula in Vol. 3. Hundreds of illustrations. Index in Vol. 3. 2000pp. 6⅛ × 9¼.   23567-X, 23568-8, 23673-0 Pa. Three-vol. set $37.85

THE ART NOUVEAU STYLE BOOK OF ALPHONSE MUCHA, Alphonse Mucha. All 72 plates from *Documents Decoratifs* in original color. Stunning, essential work of Art Nouveau. 80pp. 9⅜ × 12¼.   24044-4 Pa. $8.95

DESIGNS BY ERTE; FASHION DRAWINGS AND ILLUSTRATIONS FROM "HARPER'S BAZAR," Erte. 310 fabulous line drawings and 14 *Harper's Bazar* covers, 8 in. full color. Erte's exotic temptresses with tassels, fur muffs, long trains, coifs, more. 129pp. 9⅜ × 12¼.   23397-9 Pa. $8.95

HISTORY OF STRENGTH OF MATERIALS, Stephen P. Timoshenko. Excellent historical survey of the strength of materials with many references to the theories of elasticity and structure. 245 figures. 452pp. 5⅜ × 8½.   61187-6 Pa. $9.95

Prices subject to change without notice.

Available at your book dealer or write for free catalog to Dept. GI, Dover Publications, Inc., 31 East 2nd St. Mineola, N.Y. 11501. Dover publishes more than 175 books each year on science, elementary and advanced mathematics, biology, music, art, literary history, social sciences and other areas.